DEFAULT GOLF

Finding David

Graham Hawkings

PGA ADVANCED
COACH

Grosvenor House
Publishing Limited

This book is published by
Grosvenor House Publishing Ltd
Link House
140 The Broadway, Tolworth, Surrey, KT6 7HT.
www.grosvenorhousepublishing.co.uk

A CIP record for this book
is available from the British Library

ISBN 978-1-83975-763-1

DEDICATION

For PAT, ALFIE and SAMMY
together we make the
perfect four ball

CONTENTS

INTRODUCTION

"I sincerely apologise to all left handed golfers out there that this book is written from a right hander's perspective. However where possible I have used dexterity neutral language rather than right or left. For example for a right hander our left leg becomes our 'lead' leg, our right leg is our 'trail' leg. The same would go for a right handers left hand, that becomes our top hand, the right hand is the bottom hand." A 'slice' for a right hander become a hook, a 'fade', a draw.

DEFAULT GOLF "Finding David" Why finding David? why not finding Mark or James or Susan or Mary?

For that answer you need to look no further than that great Italian renaissance artist and sculptor Michelangelo. Who with only a bag of simple tools and a block of marble carved one of the most iconic sculptures the world has ever seen, the statue of David. There were however other unseen ingredients that went into the production of his masterpiece, there was his imagination, his vision, his desire and most of all his commitment.

You are your own block of marble, no one knows you better than yourself. In that respect you are immediately one step ahead of Michelangelo, he didn't know how that marble would carve until he started chipping away.

He had a basic set of tools, you have your own default golf swing. The aim of this book is give you the opportunity to add to your own basic tool kit the skills with which you can improve your performance.

If you can summon up the imagination, the vision and the desire and commit to the process as Michelangelo did there is no reason why you can't find your own David.

Little did I know at the time but my own journey began many many moons ago when I went off with my father Brian, my role that day was to be the dutiful son and pull his golf trolley around one of the council owned municipal golf courses of Birmingham. The usual destination for these outings was either Pype Hayes, Coxmoor Woods, Harborne Church Farm or the Lickey Hills or if you want to give, it it's posh name "Rose Hill"

Back in those days things were a little more relaxed than are now, nobody minded that much when dad threw down a ball, handed me one of his old clubs, which I hasten to add had been cut down to a more suitable length and told me to have a hit, so my golfing journey began.

Every Sunday afternoon come rain or shine there we were father and son happily swishing away enjoying not only each other's company but also the challenges that the game presented.

Looking back at those days it was definitely a case of trial and error when it came to seeking improvement, golf was hardly ever televised, if you were lucky you had the last three holes of the last round of the Open watched in glorious grainy black and white. Professional coaching was a rarity, magazines were few and far between and as for books well, those were far too boring to interest a young lad who probably thought he knew it all any way.

Fast forward to the present day and I can categorically say that we can quite easily suffer from information overload. Advice on how to "Up your game" is everywhere and all of that is great. Golf has come along way, it is at last shedding its image of being only for the upper classes. It has become much more accessible to the masses, I'm convinced that all of the advice given is well meaning, the difficulty comes when we have to sift that advice. We have to find out what is specific for our needs, in order to do that we first need to appreciate that the golf ball only acts on the information that it is given by the clubhead at that precise moment of impact.

This is where I believe "Default Golf" can be of great help, not only to the beginner and improver but also to the established player.

I wouldn't say that I believe that given long enough a Chimpanzee given a keyboard will eventually be able to write down the works of Shakespeare, but I do believe that given long enough we will figure out the best way forward for any given procedure. I myself being having been mostly self taught would have definitely improved at a faster rate had I had the benefit of professional tuition at an early age. To my way of thinking if you are committed to the process and good enough you will find a way, with professional help you taking a short cut.

There is more than one way to play this game, therefore must be more than one way to play this game WELL.

ACKNOWLEDGEMENTS

This is the part of the book where generally a huge list appears of those who have helped the author on their journey.

As someone who is largely self taught these guiding lights were never that prevalent.

However that does not mean that there hasn't been any input. As I began my golfing journey at such a young age obviously it fell upon my parents Brian and Joan and sisters Brenda and Jenny to willingly offer their support and encouragement, something for which I will be eternally grateful for.

The day that Pat my future wife walked into my life it changed for ever more, the punch I threw that day was far in excess of anything that someone of my weight should be capable of.

She instantly became my soulmate, without her love, trust and enthusiasm my life and golfing career could quite easily have quickly unravelled.

My thanks must also go out to my former boss Grahame Harris PGA Professional, AKA "Cod's" who supported me when the sharks were circling, sadly Grahame passed away a few years ago now.

I truly believe that everyone at some point in their lives come across opportunities to better themselves, some people don't see them so can't react, others see them but don't react, then there are those that see them and grasp that opportunity with both hands. I would like to think that I am firmly camped in the latter.

To that end I would like to thank Malvern College where I have been the Head Golf Coach for the last eleven years, giving a special mention to John Cox (Master i/c Golf) and The Old Malvernian Golf Society (OMGS) for their continued support.

To Ed and the team for their hospitality at Hilton Puckrup Hall, the location for the images contained in this book.

PART ONE

Non-debatable

CHAPTER 1

Finding *David*

What is *Default Golf*? *Default Golf* is all about showing you where to look to find your best performance when it comes to improving your golf. It's about sifting and filtering all sorts of input and information, finding what works and what doesn't. Some of the advice included in this book will be what I call "generic"; some of it will be "targeted".

Generic advice will come in the form of non-debatable topics such as BALL SPEED and SPIN. Targeted advice will address many of the myths and much of the confusion surrounding peoples' perceptions of how the golf club needs to be swung in order to hit good shots. For example, do we need to lift our left heel off the ground as we get to the top of the backswing, or are we better off keeping it planted? The simple answer is that it depends on the individual: someone who is less supple may well benefit from a little heel raise, as it will help create a good, powerful turn. For someone more flexible, stronger and more powerful, it may be an unnecessary addition to their swing.

Learning what works and what doesn't is a voyage of discovery for each of us; we are all individuals who not only see, hear and feel things differently to others, but also sift advice in our own unique way. What works for one person may not necessarily work for another; we need to find our own way. The longer we have been playing the more scar tissue we will have accumulated; we have to learn to look beyond this. We first need to understand what we need to do to improve, and then have to choose a route for our journey, looking beyond that scar tissue, learning to trust our decisions and committing to the process – progress not perfection.

It's similar, in a way, to when Michelangelo began to carve his masterpiece *David*. Did he just start chipping away, letting the block of marble guide him to his end result? Or was David already in there waiting to be discovered? Good question.

Let *Default Golf* become your *David*; use your default swing to guide you on a journey through your own block of marble to your *David*. We all have one inside us; it's just a matter of finding it, so start chipping away.

You will find that as you progress you will develop strengths and weaknesses. Learn to play to your strengths while all the time seeking to improve the weaknesses. Don't focus on the impossible. For instance, if you are of slight build and advancing years it is not a realistic goal to hit the ball as far as someone younger and more supple. After all, you wouldn't ask a goldfish to climb a tree. What you can do, though, is become a red-hot chipper and putter.

I'm not about to try to reinvent the wheel. Many others have attempted that and many more will try to do so. Whichever way you look at it, golf always has been and always will be just a ball-and-stick game.

The basic physics of hitting a golf ball correctly have never changed. In a nutshell, to hit a golf ball to the best of our ability we have to deliver the club head to the back of the ball with the desired face orientation and the desired speed on the desired path at the correct angle of attack.

The vast majority of golf instruction books are centred around the dos and don'ts, the whys and wherefores and how and how not to bring about the actions involved in creating the perfect golf swing.

What *Default Golf* sets out to do is give you the opportunity to reach your full potential by helping you to find YOUR optimum golf swing, not the swing of a Tour pro or the best player in your club or county, but the swing that allows YOU to deliver the club head at maximum speed on the path which YOU choose with the desired club-face orientation at the desired angle of attack.

All of the information and advice contained in this book comes tried and tested; there is nothing gimmicky or off the wall about it. Remember, it's still just a ball-and-stick game.

Most of us have driven a car but don't necessarily need to know the ins and outs of how the engine works.

What we do need to know is what impact the controls of the car have in respect to us successfully reaching our destination.

For instance, if we turn the steering wheel to the right, the car changes course and goes right. If we press the brake pedal, the car slows down or stops: cause and effect.

Similarly, we don't necessarily need to know how our body (engine) works when we swing a golf club. We do need to know what impact on our swing and consequently our ball-striking our controls (set-up, path and plane, etc.) have.

I used the examples of steering wheel and brakes in a car to highlight cause and effect. If I use the way we hold the club and ball positioning combined as an example for hitting golf shots, hopefully you will understand cause and effect within the context of hitting those shots.

If we rotate our hands to the right from a neutral position we expect the ball to go left, and vice versa. Rotating them to the left from neutral will encourage the ball to go to the right: cause and effect. Incorrect ball positioning can affect the quality of strike and the direction in which the shot goes: cause and effect.

The end product after reading and digesting the information in this book will be your own swing, a swing that allows YOU to reach YOUR optimum performance level. Along the way you will pick up the necessary information not only to help you hit great golf shots but also to become your own personal coach.

Part One covers the non-debatable questions surrounding the motion of hitting a golf ball; it looks at the physics behind what makes the golf ball react as it does when hit.

Do you need lessons to play golf? No.

Do you need lessons to play better golf? Probably yes.

The responsibility for YOUR improvement lies with yourself but tuition will certainly help.

CHAPTER 2

Default golf swing

Having coached this wonderful game now for over 30 years and played it for a good many more before that, I have probably come across most if not all the reasons behind why golfers don't hit the shots they think they ought to.

Many a time I have heard, "I lifted my head" or "I must have bent my left arm", to the more bizarre "I breathed out instead of in at the top of my backswing".

A little knowledge can be a dangerous thing, never more so than when someone with limited understanding attempts to diagnose not only their own swing but those of others too.

Probably the most common response when a client is asked why they have come for lessons is, "I want to be more consistent." People fail to realise that they are already consistent in what they are doing; it's just that they are not doing what they need to do.

Consistency comes with being habitual, so golfers need to change their bad habits into good habits. It's as simple as that.

Many of us have what I call our "default swing" – the swing with which we were born. Very rarely is this default swing the one we need to perform at our best, but what it does is gives us the basic building blocks on which we can develop a sounder method for swinging the club.

We find that to perform to our full potential one or two aspects of our default swing need altering in some way so that bad habits are swapped for good ones, maximising what our default swing has to offer.

In all my years of teaching I can probably count on the fingers of one hand the number of pupils who have had absolutely nothing going for them when they first come for a lesson. Many seem surprised when, after an initial analysis, I say that there are a lot of good things going on already. It can be anything from a technical point of view to their mental approach; very rarely does someone bring nothing to the party.

My own skeleton in the cupboard (default swing) has always been to "come over the top", a term used to describe the path the club head takes in the downswing which is above the most suitable swing plane. The opposite of this is "underneath", but more of that later in the book – not my own trials and tribulations you will be happy to know, but more information on what these terms relate to and the impact they have on our attempt to hit the ball as we wish to.

Building these new habits become easier once we have a sound understanding of what makes the golf ball do what it does once it has been hit. "Once it's been hit" is a strange thing to say, you might think, but it is only after the ball has been hit that we begin to get the feedback.

That feedback comes from touch, or, as it is sometimes referred to in golfing parlance, "feel", sight and hearing.

I'm a great believer in the power of acceptance. If we never move the club head away from the ball to begin the golf swing we will never hit a bad shot. So by moving the club away from the ball it all starts to become very risky; in beginning the backswing we start off a chain reaction – once the ball has been struck we will have any one of three responses:

a) GOOD

b) OK

c) NOT GOOD

If we are honest with ourselves, I can pretty much guarantee that there will be far more OKs and NOT GOODs than there ever will be GOODs.

Learning to accept this risk significantly helps our development. Even the top Tour pros know that somewhere in their next 18 holes they are going to have to cope with some sort of disappointment, as the shot they are intent on hitting doesn't come off. Accepting the risk makes you better prepared to deal with the outcome.

Top players spend a great deal of time practising to build new habits, to work with their "default swing".

It is the player who hits the fewest bad shots who is the better golfer, not the one who hits the best shots most often – damage limitation.

It sounds straightforward enough but therein lies the challenge. Permanent change calls for commitment and desire, both of which might also call for a change in attitude. Ask any worthwhile coach what they look for in a pupil and they will say commitment, attitude, desire, a love for the game and a willingness to learn, long before they use words such as skill and ability.

Ability comes from having skills. Skills can be learned but commitment, attitude and desire come from somewhere within us; it's impossible to find if it's not already there. But let's assume that you have the necessary desire to improve, that somewhere deep within you, you have your own *David*. Let's see if we can find him.

ABILITY is what we are capable of.
DESIRE determines what we want.
MOTIVATION determines what we do.
ATTITUDE determines how well we do it.

Chapter 3

The ball doesn't know

What doesn't the ball know? It doesn't know anything until it comes into contact with the club face. It doesn't have a pre-programmed flight path and has no idea who is holding the club that will send it on its journey. It could be the world number one player; it could be a complete beginner. It only reacts to the laws of physics.

In the split second in which the club face comes into contact with the ball it gives it all the information it requires to reach its destination.

This information comes in four guises and each contributes in its own way, although there may well be some overlap.

a) SPEED

b) DIRECTION

c) LAUNCH ANGLE

d) SPIN

Let's have a brief look at each of these four factors. More in-depth information will come later.

SPEED = distance

The two main contributors to how fast the ball leaves the club face are club-head speed and where on the club face the ball is struck.

The more club-head speed we generate the further the ball will go, but only if the ball is struck in the middle of a club face, which is square to the path on which it is travelling. An off-centre strike will lose ball speed. Therefore, there is a trade-off between club-head speed and the ability of the player to constantly find the middle of the club face.

We must also factor in a strike carried out with a club face either open or closed to the path on which it is travelling. Hit with an open face and the ball will lose speed; a closed face will add speed. Overlap here with SPIN.

DIRECTION = accuracy

To understand how accuracy is achieved we first need to appreciate that golf is played in circles. First of all, we have a "round" of golf, the ball is "round", the hole is "round". In this respect we also have to understand that the golf swing is a circle, that the club head moves in a circular direction around the body.

Where the club face is pointing on impact has the largest influence on where the ball goes. I would like to add here that the only time the club face needs to be pointing to the target is the moment of impact. Should the face be pointing to the target at any other time during the swing it will be either open or closed to the path. This is because, as previously mentioned, the path that the club head takes is circular.

Depending on which set of statistics you care to believe the club face has somewhere between a 70 and 80 per cent influence on the initial direction in which the ball leaves the club face. The remaining 20 to 30 per cent comes from the path on which the club head is travelling combined with club-face orientation.

Club-face orientation will be square, open or closed.

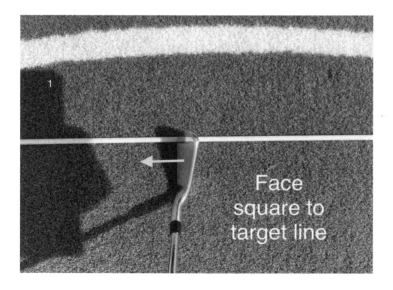

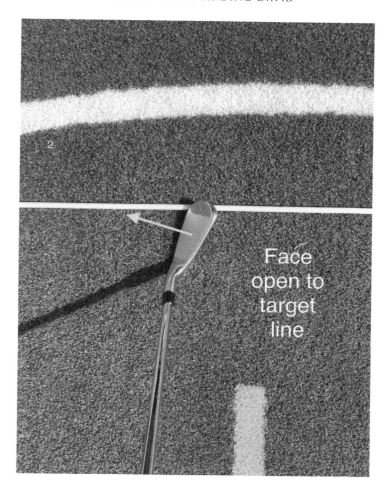

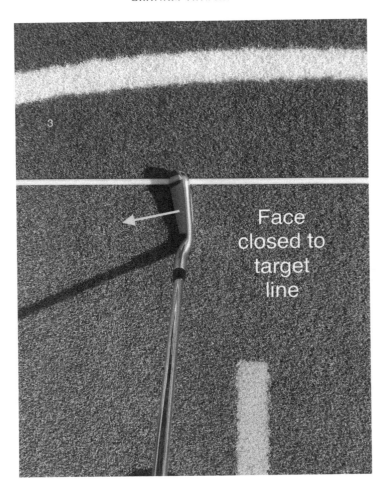

Face
closed to
target
line

Marry them to swing path, which will be in-to-out, out-to-in or in-to-in, gives us the direction and shape of the ball flight.

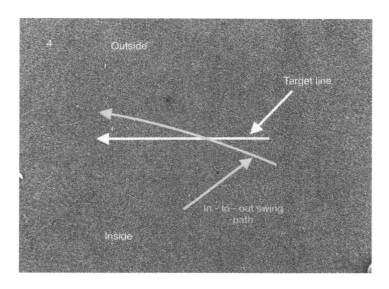

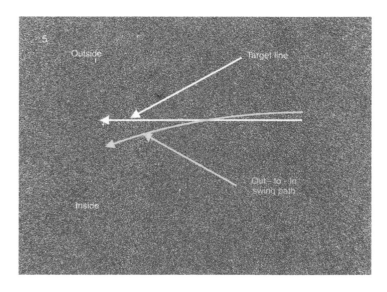

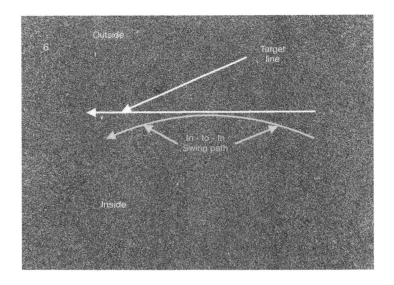

A ball hit with a face that is square to the path on which it is travelling will always go in a straight line.

A ball hit with a face that is open to the path will always curve to the right. Overlap with SPIN.

A ball that is hit with a face that is closed to the path will always curve to the left. Overlap with SPIN.

From these combinations we can safely accept that there are nine possible ball flights for each shot. Golf is hard!

LAUNCH ANGLE = trajectory

The biggest influence on launch angle is the loft on the club face. If asked the question, most people assume that the most lofted club will hit the ball the highest and the least lofted the lowest. This sounds logical. But no, this is not the case. What these people don't realise is that a consistently well-struck shot will peak at around the same height regardless of the club being used. If you give yourself around a 10 per cent window of dispersion in maximum height from club to club, count yourself among the more talented ball strikers.

It is the launch angle that varies from club to club: the greater the loft, the steeper the launch angle.

We also have what we call "dynamic loft". This is the actual loft angle that is presented to the ball on impact. This is usually lower than the actual loft set on the club face by the manufacturer, due to the fact that the ball is hit with a descending blow – with irons, anyway.

With a driver we are looking to hit the ball with a rising club head. Therefore, in this case, we add loft at impact.

Another impact on launch angle is club-face orientation. An open face which adds loft will launch the ball higher; a closed face which decreases loft will launch the ball lower than what we might think of as the "optimum" launch angle. Overlap here with DIRECTION and SPIN.

SPIN = control

Every shot is influenced by the spin that has been imparted on the ball by the club face. You may have noticed that spin overlaps into all other criteria affecting ball-flight laws, so learning how and what spin is imparted is paramount to being able to read your ball flight and then make the necessary adjustments.

There are two spin orientations for golf shots (not counting putting). There is side spin, which is either clockwise, causing the ball to curve to the right, or anti-clockwise, which causes the ball to curve to the left. Then there is backspin, which helps to get the ball airborne and maintain its flight until landing, where it then aids stopping the ball. Master and control spin, be it side or backspin, and you are well on the way to controlling your ball flight.

PART TWO

Debatable

CHAPTER 1

Jigsaw

How technically correct do we have to be to play the game well?

It's safe to assume that the more orthodox we can become, the better are our chances of reaching our potential. But you only have to look at the world's top players to find that a great many of them put their own personal slant on the golf swing so that it produces the desired results. They have found their *David*.

They are each in their own way what we might classify as "outliers", taking their unique route to maximise their potential.

Two such players come to mind, one from a bygone era, the other an exponent of the more modern game: Ben Hogan, who said "the secret is in the dirt", and Bryson de Chambeau, who takes a more scientific approach to playing and who found a lot of his answers in data and statistics.

One thing you can be sure of is that both these great players committed to the process of improving. They did their 10,000 hours or more of structured practice. They had DESIRE, they were MOTIVATED and they had great ATTITUDE.

History is littered with like-minded golfers: Moe Norman, Seve Ballesteros, Jack Nicklaus and Tiger Woods all found their way to doing it.

Unfortunately, there are also those who lost their way when moving away from the default swing, such as Ian Baker Finch, the Australian, who, for some reason, thought that after winning the British Open his game still wasn't good enough, so set about changing his method. He was never heard of again. Another is Martin Kymer, the German player, who, after becoming world number one playing his way, thought he needed to change from fading the ball to drawing it. It took him years to get back to anything like the player he was. By the way, he is now back to fading it . Luke Donald, the Englishman, also reached world number one playing his way, not that long, but solid and straight off the tee with a red-hot short game. He began to lose his way by trying to hit the ball longer.

All these players found their *David*, only to lose it by trying things that didn't fit with their default swing.

I think it's pretty safe to assume that you have had a go at playing, and, dare I say it, have already formed a certain amount of the scar tissue I spoke of earlier. You are now on the quest for some sort of help and improvement.

I can guarantee that if you do the simple things well, improvement will follow close behind.

I'm guessing that at some point in our lives we have all tackled a jigsaw puzzle. It is pretty well an unwritten rule that you begin the puzzle by working around the edges, starting from a corner (if it has them).

This method gives us the best opportunity to build the complete picture, and with golf, a sound set-up is the equivalent of getting the corners of our jigsaw puzzle in place. If we take how we aim the club, hold the club, stand to the ball and position the ball, as the four corners of our jigsaw we are well on our way.

Learn from good players. Good players have fewer difficult shots to hit than their lesser counterparts. Great players have fewer still. Higher handicapped golfers end up with a lot of very challenging shots to hit. It's ironic that the better player you become the easier are the shots you are left with. You hit more shots from the fairway, you play fewer shots from the rough or trees, and you have fewer bunker shots: cause and effect.

So what do all great players do?

Most have a good orthodox set-up. This is something that any able-bodied person can achieve. They also have the ability to deliver the club head on plane in the downswing to the back of the ball. This is something that any able-bodied person can achieve. Flexibility might be a concern but all that this means is that your swing may be a little shorter and slower than someone more agile.

Get your set-up sorted and learn to swing on plane and you will be well on the way to finding *David*. Learn to do the simple things well!

AIM (the club face)

As mentioned earlier the ball will go where the club face is pointing at the moment of impact, so let's get the face aimed correctly to begin with.

In order to do this, place the club head on the ground with its leading edge (bottom front edge) "square" or at 90 degrees to the direction in which you want the ball to go. This direction is called the "ball-to-target line".

Everything from here on in this book is suggested to help you return the club head into this position at the precise moment of impact. Aim the face to the right of target and it is "open", to the left and it is "closed".

A ball hit with a face that is "open" to the path on which it is travelling will always curve to the right. If it is hit with a face that is "closed" to the path it will always curve to the left. If the face is "square" to the path it will fly straight.

HOLD

The most important golf lesson anyone will ever have is the one in which they are shown how to place their hands on the golf club in order to deliver the face to the ball with their chosen club-face orientation. This will be either square, open or closed; the choice is yours. Therefore, this is probably the most important chapter in this book.

So many of the lessons I have given seem to begin with an explanation of why the club should be held in a certain way. I have seen so many "light-bulb moments" from pupils after initiating just a small change in the way they hold the club once they understand the implications of what they are doing.

A good "hold" on the club won't guarantee a good shot, but it will give you a better chance than a bad hold, which will probably encourage a bad shot. You may have already noticed that I use the words "hold" and "place" rather than "grip" when describing our hands and their relationship with the club.

"Grip" to me sends out the wrong message. Ask someone to grip something and instinctively they grab it with tension. Ask them to "hold" it and the message is quite different. Their hold is softer, more relaxed, tension free. If in doubt try a simple experiment: pick up and hold an egg. Your fingers, hand and arm will be tension free and you will be able to move your wrist, bend your elbow and wave your arm around without breaking the egg.

Imagine the consequences of then gripping the egg; it all gets very messy, very quickly!

I recommend a sliding scale of one to 10 to describe the pressure with which you should hold the club. This seems to work well and is easily understood. A value of one is very loose; you feel you could drop the club. In contrast, 10 is as tight as you can. A value of around four tends to suit most people; seven and above and you are making omelettes.

Before you build your preferred hold, understand that your hands will perform better by working as a unit. This is best achieved by having the palms of your hands facing one another. Clap your hands in front of you so that your fingers point down to the ground. With your hands in this position and feet, knees, hips and shoulders parallel to the ball-to-target line, the back of your left hand and the palm of your right hand should be facing the target.

This position is called "neutral" and gives you the best opportunity to present the club face squarely onto the back of the ball.

Remember, a face that is square to the path will always hit the ball in a straight line. Any deviation from this neutral positioning of the hands will make it more difficult to hit the ball straight. We can still play if our hands are rotated together so that palms still face each other in either a clockwise or anti-clockwise direction on the grip of the club. It's just less likely that we will hit the ball straight. In rotating the hands clockwise we are "strengthening" the hold; anti-clockwise we are weakening the hold. It is important, here, to fully understand that terminology.

The terms "strengthen" and "weaken" in this instance refer to the positioning of the hands, not the tension with which we hold the club. The terms "strong" and "weak" are derived from the type of shot we expect to hit with the hands in the designated position. A "strong" hold on the club will encourage a right-to-left ball flight, which is a more penetrating shot than the weaker left-to-right ball flight that we would expect from a weaker hold in which the hands have rotated in an anti-clockwise direction away from "neutral".

The two suggested ways of linking your hands together are to have the little finger of your bottom hand overlapping or interlocking with the forefinger of your top hand.

Neutral hold, back of left hand facing target

NEUTRAL
STRONG
WEAK hold on club

The key to building a solid hold on the club is to correctly place your top hand on the club. If correctly positioned the grip of the club should sit in the crook of the forefinger and across your hand to point opposite the base of your thumb. Also, the fleshy pad at the base of the hand will sit on top of the grip.

A simple check to ensure that the top hand is in a suitable position is to hold the club with the top hand only, with it resting in the crook of the forefinger with no other fingers touching the club.

With the fleshy part of your hand on top of the grip you should be able to hinge your wrist up and down without the club slipping across your palm.

10

Correct positioning of the left hand allows for natural hingeing of the wrist

The thumb of the top hand runs down the top right centre of the grip, not down the top middle. The bottom hand comes in from the side so that the palm of the hand faces the target, either interlocking or overlapping the little finger of your bottom hand with the forefinger of your top hand.

Wrap the hand over the grip so that the thumb of the top hand sits comfortably in the palm of the bottom hand. The thumb of the bottom hand runs down the centre left of the grip. The grip of the club should now be running over the base of the fingers of the bottom hand.

If the above is followed and the club face is correctly aimed from square on to the target line, we should be able to hinge our wrists, lifting the club head up in front of us, to see that the leading edge is vertical. If the leading edge is running off to the right, towards where 1 o'clock would be, the face is open; going back towards 11 o'clock and the face is closed. Vertical, 12 o'clock, it is square.

So there we have it, an in-depth look at how best to hold the club and how it affects the delivery of the club face.

To reiterate, this is the most important golf lesson any one can have. Take time to learn and understand the importance of placing your hands on the club so that you create the ball flight you desire.

Experiment with a neutral, strong and weak hold, and be mindful of how these different holds can impact shoulder alignment. A weak hold may open your shoulders to the target, pointing them left, a strong hold possibly closes them, pointing them to the right of the target.

CHAPTER 2

The low point

Good solid ball striking calls for an ability to consistently put the low point of the swing in the correct place each time.

To compress the ball with irons, the ball needs to be hit with a descending blow. This should put the low point marginally towards the target from where the ball sits on the ground. With the driver the ball needs to be hit with an ascending blow, therefore the low point of the swing needs to be marginally behind the ball which is sat on a tee peg.

The problem here, though, can begin with a changing low point. You need to appreciate that the low point of the swing changes very marginally from club to club.

As the length of a club changes, the driver being the longest and the wedge the shortest, so does the angle of descent or ascent of the club head coming into the ball relative to the ground. The wedge swing will have a steeper, V-shaped angle of attack, as opposed to a driver swing, which will resemble a U shape.

The V-shaped swing of the wedge calls for a very precise judgement of the low point. The middle of the stance is always a good place to start when positioning the ball for a standard wedge shot. This places the ball directly in front of the sternum, which represents the centre of the body. It is fairly safe to assume that as we swing the club to the right (backswing) and to the left (follow through) the low point will be in the middle.

As the clubs from the wedge get physically longer so the shape of our swing alters. Going from a wedge to nine, eight, seven, six irons, etc. will be gradually moving the shape of our swing from V-shaped to U-shaped. Therefore, the ball must be moved increasingly further forward incremental to the change of club.

The easiest way to check where the low point of your swing falls is by checking your divots. A divot behind the ball is a result of a swing bottoming out too early. The result of this is a ball that is hit "fat". Poor weight transfer is one of the major reasons for people having difficulty in obtaining a consistent low point.

Another possibility is that the ball is positioned too far forward to begin with, leaving the low point behind the ball.

A simple practice drill to help move the low point forward is to place your golf towel or something similar approximately 6in behind the ball. The challenge is to strike the ball avoiding contact with the towel, and then move it increasingly closer to the ball as your skill levels increase.

CHAPTER 3

The circle

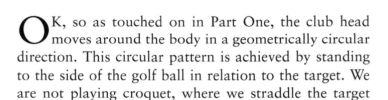

OK, so as touched on in Part One, the club head moves around the body in a geometrically circular direction. This circular pattern is achieved by standing to the side of the golf ball in relation to the target. We are not playing croquet, where we straddle the target line, nor is it cricket, which is played very much up and down the line.

The only time in a golf swing that the club face needs to look at the target is the precise moment of impact. Coming into ball, the club face is looking to the right of target; a split second after impact the face will begin to look to the left of target, assuming, that is, that we are attempting to hit the ball straight.

We are now beginning to move towards appreciating how our body alignment can affect the path on which the club head travels on its journey around the body. Optimum body alignment places our shoulders, hips, knees and feet parallel to the ball-to-target line.

Imagine standing on a railway track with your feet placed on one of the rails and the ball positioned on the other, the railway sleeper on which the rails sit forming our right angle, which equates to the leading edge of the club face being squared to the target line.

Deviating from this, this alignment makes it less likely that you will deliver the club head along the most suitable target line.

Most people whom I have had the pleasure to coach have always seemed to prioritise the alignment of their feet over their shoulders. Might I suggest here that we change that priority and make our shoulders the main focus of attention when lining up.

The only contact we have with the club is with our hands. Our hands are connected to our arms and our arms to our shoulders, and if we have our shoulders parallel to the target line we can swing the club along the preferred target line of in-to-in, REGARDLESS of where our feet are pointing. The club head does not cross the ball-to-target line. Aligning the shoulders either to the left of target (open) or to the right (closed) encourages either an out-to-in or in-to-out swing path. Our "circle" has now become misaligned and the club head will now be crossing the ball-to-target line.

Of course, shoulder alignment that is either open or closed can be used on purpose to alter the swing path if we wish to manufacture a particular ball flight, especially when matched to the relevant hold on the club: NEUTRAL for a straight ball flight, WEAK for a left-to-right ball flight, STRONG for a right-to-left ball flight.

The concept of having the shoulders lined up correctly allows for the optimum swing path to be created. The alignment of the hips, knees and feet allows for a balanced swing to be made either side of the golf ball, where a good upper-body turn away from the target creating the backswing loads our weight onto our right side.

After a good transition in which our weight is shifted from our right side onto our left side the downswing is initiated, culminating in a fast body turn towards the target and ending up in a balanced upright position facing the target, our body weight stacked over our left foot.

In a nutshell "two turns and a swish".

CHAPTER 4

Golf in the "V"

All good golfers have the ability to swing the club "on plane", but what is "on plane" and why is it crucial to the correct delivery of the club head?

Quite simply, the plane is the angle at which the club is swung when moving in its circular travels around the body relative to the ground. For example, the wheels of your car rotate on a vertical plane and the plate inside your microwave oven rotates on a horizontal plane.

We all have our individual optimum swing plane, but not only one. We have a separate swing plane for each club we use. This might well sound confusing; don't worry, it isn't.

If we achieve a good posture position when getting set up, by standing at a comfortable distance from the ball, our arms hanging down in a relaxed manner and with the necessary spine angle created by tilting forward from the hips, we have set our swing plane.

However, not only do we have our swing plane we also have what we call "shaft plane". This is the angle of the golf shaft relative to the ground. The separation between these two planes automatically generates a sort of tilted letter "V". Keeping the club head somewhere between these two plane lines, both in the backswing and downswing, greatly improves our chance of delivering the club head into the ball successfully.

16

Shaft plane also changes from club to club

Swing plane line runs from ball up through Sternum. It will change slightly from club to club

To recognise your swing plane when looking down the line of the shot towards the target simply draw a line from the ball through a point on your body just below where you would tie a necktie at the top of your sternum. This line is our "optimum swing plane". The reason that this alters from club to club and individual to individual is:

a) With a driver we are standing further away from the ball than with a wedge. Therefore, our spine angle will be a little more upright. Both swing and shaft plane angle will be "flatter" or "shallower".

We tilt over from the hips more when using shorter clubs, which means that both swing and shaft planes become more "upright" or "steeper".

b) A taller person will have more spine angle tilt than a shorter person and, therefore, a steeper, more upright plane.

18

Left arm, back of left hand, and clubface all parallel to one another

Swing plane for driver

This swing plane line acts as a valuable reference for getting the club set correctly at the top of the backswing and moving the club through the most advantageous positions in the backswing and downswing.

To get the club "on plane" in the backswing let me walk you through a couple of simple swing motions.

First of all, from our neutral set-up position on the railway tracks move the club away from the ball low to the ground and slightly on the inside of the target line (remember the circle). This move of the club head away from the ball should be initiated by a turning of the shoulders coupled with a slight rotation of the forearms. Imagine your arms and the shaft of the club forming a letter Y. The letter-Y relationship should if possible be maintained until the club shaft reaches horizontal and is on a line that places it directly above the railway track on which your feet are placed, provided we can maintain a connection between the upper part of arms and our core.

What is "connection"? you might ask. It is maintaining the relationship between our arms and the upper part of our body so that they work in unison. Failure to maintain this relationship is one of the prime reasons why golfers find it difficult to swing on plane. Connection allows us to keep the club in front of our chest, maintaining the letter Y. Losing connection often happens as a result of the club being picked up too steeply on the "outside" as the arms separate from the chest, or because there has been an over-aggressive rolling open of the hands and forearms in the backswing. This leads to a swing that is too much on the "inside" and underneath the plane.

A swing that loses connection might well be described as one in which the tail is wagging the dog instead of the dog wagging the tail, as the arms tend to work with too much independence.

A simple practice drill to build connection, which has been around for many years in some shape or form, is to place some sort of small object – anything from a leaf to a towel – into the armpit of each arm. Hold it in place with the upper arms and swing them slowly in a small arc, keeping the object in place. Gradually build to a full swing.

This will feel very restrictive to begin with, but please persevere. Doing so could really be a game changer if you are seeking a more consistent method. A disconnected golf swing turns our circle into "buckled wheel".

Having moved the club back to this "halfway" position as described, we should find that if the golf shaft were the barrel of a gun the bullet would come out of the grip end of the club and go straight towards the target.

If the head of the club is "outside" the hands, we are too steep in the backswing and over the top of the swing plane, and the bullet will go left of target.

If the club head is "inside" the hands we are too shallow in the backswing and underneath the shaft plane, and the bullet will be going right of target.

19

Clubhead
outside of
hands and
target line
also above
swing plane

It is possible to play with both "over the top" and "underneath" swings with the correct manipulation of the club face. This manipulation is manufactured via a deviation in the club-face orientation, by way of either a "stronger" or "weaker" hold on the club.

With the club shaft on a line above our toes with shaft horizontal to the ground, how do we know that its face is square? With that slight forearm rotation we spoke of, simply match the leading edge to the angle of your spine and the face will be square. If the leading edge is vertical (toe up) the face will be open, and if it is looking down to the ground (toe down) the face will be closed.

Clubshaft and left arm on target line with face matching spine angle, clubhead nicely set between swing and shaft plane

22

Face open in
backswing -
Toe up

It from here that we will look at what many feel is the next stage of building the backswing. This is what is commonly known as "wrist break" or "cocking the wrists" and is the hinging of the wrist that allows the club to remain "on plane", with the face square for the completion of the backswing.

If we go back to our original set-up position with the club grounded behind the ball, the correct wrist action is one that allows the club head to be picked up vertically away from the ball using only our wrists. If done correctly, with the club head out in front of us, this will place the leading edge of the club in a vertical position. Imagine a clock face. If the leading edge is vertical it is at 12 o'clock and therefore "square". If it is veering towards 11 or even 10 o'clock, it is "closed". If it veers towards 1 or 2 o'clock, it is "open".

Should the club face end up in either of the closed or open positions I suggest you check that your hold on the club is neutral. Refer to images 12, 13 and 14.

To reiterate, a "strong" hold on the club will encourage a closed club face and therefore a right-to-left ball flight, and a "weak" hold will encourage the opposite – an open face and a left-to-right ball flight. A "neutral" hold will give you a square club face and a straight ball flight.

Unbeknown to many is the fact that we have already preset a certain amount of wrist break when addressing the ball. In a comfortable set-up position with our arms hanging relaxed from our shoulders, an obtuse angle is created between our arms and the club shaft. This angle is created by a small amount of wrist break.

The completion of the wrist break takes place somewhere around the waist high area that the club moves through as mentioned previously.

Delaying the wrist break until we are well into the backswing allows us to maintain "width", which helps to create club-head speed. As the shoulders continue to turn away from the target, the arm swing incorporating the wrist break brings the club into a position somewhere above our right shoulder, with the shaft once again parallel to the target line.

If we are "on plane", the left arm incorporating the back of left hand and the leading edge of the club head should be parallel to one another on the same plane line that we had at address. The line is then an extension of the one from the ball up through our chest to the top of our sternum.

18

Left arm, back of left hand, and clubface all parallel to one another

Swing plane for driver

In a nutshell

The three key moves it takes to achieve the optimum top of the backswing position in preferential order are:

a) Shoulder turn.
b) Forearm rotation.
c) Wrist break.

The end result from the advice above should be a coiled, powerfully athletic position, with our body weight loaded onto our right leg.

To help ensure the correct sequencing of weight transference it might be worth investing in a homemade device that I call a "weight-shift board". Find yourself a piece of plywood approximately 30in (75cm) by 12in (30cm). Across the short side in the centre fix to this a piece of wood measuring 2in by 1in (50cm by 25cm). A see-saw motion will be generated when you stand on the board and turn your body to the right for the backswing then left for the follow through.

The swing plane – downswing

With the correct sequencing the completion of the backswing becomes the beginning of the downswing. Good sequencing calls for good rhythm.

The words "rhythm", "tempo" and suchlike are frequently used to describe the sequence of the golf swing. But what is the correct rhythm?

As with the swing plane it is personal to each individual, so therefore debatable. A person who tends to have a quick metabolism, i.e. walks quickly, talks quickly etc., will have a faster rhythm than someone who tends to do things at a slower pace.

The ideal rhythm tends to occur when we have a ratio of three:one for speed of backswing to downswing. Believe it or not this three:one ratio was established when some dedicated individuals counted frames of video film and found that one thing common to all the great golf club swingers is that they used three times as many frames in their backswings as they did in their downswings. Note that I say "great golf club swingers" not the greatest players.

We regard the backswing as being a chain-reaction series of movements that begins with the movement of the club head away from the ball initiated by our letter Y. The hands begin moving and the motion flows up through the shoulders and down through our core, triggering the hips, which are responding to the shoulder turn, our legs and finally ending in our feet.

That sequencing results in a turn of the body away from the target and a transference of weight onto our "trail" leg and ideally onto the inside of the right foot.

If we follow all of the above we might end up with a certain amount of lifting off the ground of the left heel. This is perfectly acceptable and is probably dependent on how supple we are.

The lifting of the left heel will allow the hips to turn a little more than would otherwise be possible, which in turn allows the shoulders more freedom to turn fully.

If the backswing is completed by a lifting of the left heel, the downswing begins with the replanting of it. The see-saw effect of the weight transfer board could be of use here. If the sequencing for the downswing is a reversal of the motion used to create the backswing it might well go something like this: replant the left heel. This triggers the left knee which fires the hips and in turn unwinds the shoulders. The arms drop and the wrists uncock, accelerating the club head to its maximum speed just after impact.

It is important to understand that any attempt to get the club head to reach maximum speed AT impact will most probably result in deceleration. To put it another way, hit through the ball not at it.

If carried out in the right sequence, the faster we do this the further we will hit the ball, providing we hit it in the middle of the club face.

Experience tells us that there is always a trade-off, that it can become a bit of a juggling act balancing club-head speed against our ability to find the middle of the club face. What are we going to sacrifice – head speed or strike quality?

I know which I prefer for myself, but the choice is yours. Do you want to throw everything at it but run the risk of a higher percentage of mishits, or be a bit more of a "steady Eddie" and maybe sacrifice a little distance to probably be more accurate.

As a coach I feel it is my job to give you the tools and the advice on how best to use them, but the final decision has to be yours.

One of the things that soon struck me as a coach is that people get their enjoyment in all sorts of ways. Some like to hit the ball as hard and as far as possible, regardless of the consequences; others prefer to adopt a more tactical approach, playing within themselves and plotting their way around the course. There are also those who prefer chipping and putting, while some just go for the exercise and social aspect of the game.

It is not for me to tell them what to do to get their enjoyment; it is my job as a coach to help them enjoy what they do!

As I said at the start of the book, the underlying theme is to put YOU in charge.

If we manage to follow the correct sequencing we will find that, during the transition from backswing into downswing, there will be an automatic re-routing of the club as it drops onto a shallower swing plane than the plane generated in the backswing. This re-routing ensures that the club head is swung into the impact area on an inside path. Failure to begin the downswing with the correct sequencing will most probably result in some sort of upper-body movement that throws the club onto a downswing plane higher than our optimum plane, and brings the club into the impact area at a steeper angle and from the outside.

This most often happens when the shoulders initiate the downswing by turning to the left before the lower body-weight transfer takes place. It is damaging to the delivery of the club head and has an impact on where the low point of the swing falls.

Can we play effectively with both an over-the-top swing plane and a shallower downswing? Within reason, yes. Golf is not about making perfect swings. It is about playing shots that get the ball around the course in the fewest number of strokes. There are no points for style; that is ice skating. It is about performance, and that comes down to the lowest number that you can possibly write on the scorecard.

To help you swing the club at maximum speed here's a great practice drill.

Take your normal stance, but instead of holding the club conventionally, turn it upside down so that you are holding it by the hosel, which is where the shaft and head are joined.

Then, holding the club in one hand only – I suggest the right hand to begin with – make one-handed swings, generating as much of a whooshing noise as you can with the grip end of the club. The louder the "whoosh" the faster the club head is travelling. When you feel you have reached the maximum noise with swings, change to the left hand and repeat. More noise more speed!

The through swing – shake hands

Does the through swing have a plane? Yes it does, but it is a consequence of what has gone on before so it doesn't make too many headlines, as the ball has already left the club face and is on its way.

Without a through swing, though, there would be no release and delivery of the club head. Try it: make a full backswing, loading fully onto your right side. Then, after a good transition of weight onto your left side, begin accelerating the club head towards the impact area. The correct sequencing will activate the larger muscles of your legs, back and shoulders, which in turn will activate your arms, rotating the forearms and wrists, squaring the club head. All of this movement and momentum creates a fully balanced and poised finish to the swing.

What the through swing helps to tell us, though, is whether we are transferring our weight effectively and whether we have maintained "connection" and therefore control of the club face via the necessary forearm rotation. Does the swing have a good rhythm to it so that we can complete it in a nice balanced position?

I won't add any more here because all the criteria necessary for a good through swing are analysed elsewhere in this book.

I have always found that a good reference point for checking that things are as they should be is the halfway point of the follow through.

As the body turns, with the weight being transferred onto the lead leg, we should be getting somewhere near the "shake hands" position. This means that, when the club shaft is reaching horizontal and pointing to the target, your hands will be out in front of your chest and the palm of your right hand will be vertical with your fingers if taken off the club pointing to the target, elbows relaxed. The leading edge should also be vertical to match your spine angle, as if you had turned to face the target to shake hands with it.

26

Soft relaxed elbows help with touch, feel and rhythm

CHAPTER 5

Impact – if in doubt, give it a clout

All the coaching and all the practice comes down to this and as a coach you have be very mindful of the information you pass on.

If I have nothing to say at any particular point in a lesson, so be it. Or it might be a case of reinforcing all that we have worked on before – call it maintenance or revision. A coach, however, needs to have more than one way of getting a message across.

For example, a pupil wants to learn how to manufacture a right-to-left ball flight.

A coach can go through the technical detail of how to hold the club and the effect that that has on club-face orientation; through how strengthening the hold will encourage a closing club face; and through how moving the ball back in the stance can affect the shoulder alignment, creating an in-to-out swing path. The end result should be the desired shot shape but as this doesn't always happen, you need something else.

How about a "topspin forehand" then? Can a pupil visualise what a tennis racket should do to create this shot, how the racket head should roll over the ball as it strikes it?

Or how about football and an in-swinging corner-kick from the left touchline: how the football is hit with the inside of the boot to impart that anti-clockwise spin that we know will make the ball curve left.

What these examples do, I hope, is give some indication of how controlling the spin gives us control of the ball, be it golf, tennis or football. Cast your mind back to Part 1 Non-debatable and SPIN = control.

By understanding what the club head should be doing at the precise moment of IMPACT we are more than halfway towards controlling the shot.

So many pupils come to me with an honest but misguided idea of what is required to hit a golf ball well.

They ponder about a straight left arm, or keeping their head down, or feel that in order to be a good golfer you have to draw the ball. The list goes on. They don't seem to realise that all that is needed is an understanding of what the club face should be doing at impact to achieve their desired ball flight. If they can grasp that, they are in control.

If we follow the straightforward path of correctly aiming the club face, holding the club in the described manner so that our hands are together as one unit aligned with the club face, addressing the ball in a neutral position and swinging the club on our optimum plane, golf can become a simple game – not an easy game, but a simple one. Golf never has been and never will be an exact science.

Compression

A great indicator of how good a ball striker you are comes from your ability to "compress" the ball. This compressing or squashing of the ball against the club face is one of the major factors in creating a solid strike. There is a different sound to the contact.

With iron shots, the ball is hit with a descending blow and is momentarily squeezed between club face and the ground. The easiest way to achieve this compression is to ensure that the grip end of the club is still ahead of the club face at impact; any early release of the club will reduce the opportunity to compress the ball.

To get the feeling of what compression entails simply preset your impact position. By this I mean take a middle iron and adopt your normal set-up position. From there, push your hands a couple of inches forward towards the target. This will create forward shaft lean, bringing your club shaft into a position where it forms more of a straight line with your lead (left) arm. At the same time, shift your body weight onto your lead (left) leg. Now shift your trail (right) knee towards the target, raising your right heel off the ground a little. Turn your shoulders and hips to the left, opening up your body to the target.

27

Pre - set impact. Lead arm and shaft in line, hands ahead of clubhead

For a high-launching drive, widen the stance so that the distance BETWEEN your two feet is similar to that of your shoulders. It is important that you appreciate that the width of stance is the distance between your feet, not the distance from the outside of one foot and the outside of the other. This allows your lower body to form a stable platform to support a powerful upper-body motion.

Position the ball opposite your left toe, which can be turned out towards the target a little or "flared". This may be a little further forward than is often suggested, but remember, we are trying to encourage more of an upward strike on the ball. Then, "tilt" your upper body from your hips away from the target. This will set your head back behind the ball and create a small amount of negative shaft lean. Your hands should now be behind the ball a little. It would also be advantageous at this stage to turn your head slightly to the right so that you are looking at the ball more out of your left eye.

Ideally, if we drew a line up the inside of our lead (left) leg it would continue at the same angle up through our spine and head. The right shoulder should now be lower than the left. This angled shoulder line will once again encourage an upward strike.

28

Upward strike with driver, left foot flared, spine leaning away from target, right shoulder lowered ball well forward in stance

PART THREE

Play shots, don't make swings

CHAPTER 1

See the field

The year 2000 saw the release of a Twentieth Century Fox film *The Legend of Bagger Vance*, directed by Robert Redford and starring Will Smith, Matt Damon and Charlize Theron.

It follows the early years of a soldier, Rannulph Junuh (Matt Damon), and his coming to terms with life following traumatic experiences during World War One. He is a talented amateur golfer and is taken under the wing of a mystical character called Bagger Vance (Will Smith), who caddies for him in a challenge match against the legendary Bobby Jones and Walter Hagen, staged at the opening of a new golf complex during America's Great Depression.

Rannulph has tremendous trouble dealing with his emotions and the pressure put on him to do well as the local hero, but a turning point comes when Bagger tells him to watch Bobby Jones. "Watch his eyes, look at him, searching for that one authentic golf swing", he says, as Jones makes practice swings staring down the fairway, almost as if he is willing the ball to go there regardless.

Bobby Jones duly sends his ball long and straight down the middle of the fairway. Rannulph then steps up to play his tee shot with Baggers' words ringing in his ears.

For a brief moment Rannulph is in a bubble and all his demons are banished. All that is in his mind is the ball and the fairway (the target). He lets his authentic swing take over and the ball goes down the centre of the fairway past Jones's. It is Hollywood, after all.

Rannulph finds his authentic swing, or, to put it another way, relies on his default swing to find his *David*.

"Seeing the field" is probably better known as having a pre-shot routine.

A few pages ago I said that a round of golf needed to be played by "playing shots" not by "making swings". How does that work?

In order to hit our best possible golf shot at any given time we first need to have a plan for the shot in hand, our "pre-shot routine 1" (PSR1).

This is a mental and physical routine we go through prior to hitting every shot. It puts us in a mental BUBBLE, free of outside influence. The more experienced we are, the easier this will be to achieve, as most golfers have a memory bank of what has or has not worked for them in the past.

Building a PSR is very individual but what we find is that they contain very similar content. Let us go through these universal contents.

The whole purpose of hitting a golf shot is to make the next one as easy possible. Please re-read this sentence and learn to appreciate that playing good golf is all about damage limitation. It's about hitting shots that put the ball in the best position from which to hit the next one and is quite often called "course management".

We need something to trigger our PSR1 and I suggest something simple – shall we say the putting on of our golf glove. Once we have done this we have activated our PSR1. We then analyse the shot we are faced with and choose the club to hit that shot. Tee shots are more straight forward, as the ball has a perfect lie each time, but subsequent shots may be more tricky as the way the ball is lying will have the biggest impact on club selection. Notice that I say it is the lie of the ball that has the biggest impact on club selection, not the distance you need to cover. Too many times I have seen players struggle to hit good golf shots simply because they have made a poor choice of club, usually by being over ambitious for both their and the club's capabilities.

Once the club has been chosen, stand a few paces behind the ball looking straight down the target line, and switch your vision from ball to target and back two or three times. This will imprint the target in your subconscious. I will add here that the target chosen must be as small as possible. If it is a tee shot, look down the fairway, and pick a precise spot, or maybe choose something in the far distance, e.g. a tree. And don't just aim at the tree, see if you can pick out a particular branch. Or if it's a building, pick out a particular part of the building, maybe a window, and reduce that to a pane of glass.

If you aim at a bunker in the distance choose a precise part of it – left edge or right edge, for example.

The idea behind this is that the smaller the target, the smaller the miss. This type of thinking crosses over from sport to sport: a tennis player will lay down a handkerchief in the service box to aim at; a bowler in cricket will practice bowling at just one stump; a footballer, when taking a penalty, will pick out one square of the netting in the back of the goal to aim at. The smaller the target, the smaller the miss.

Next, pick a spot on the ground on the ball-to-target line and maybe a couple of yards ahead. Use it as an intermediate target to line up with. It is easier to line up with something a lot closer than something a few hundred yards away.

Still standing, so that you are looking down the target line, use your imagination and visualisation skills to run a video of yourself hitting the shot you have chosen,

Step into the video, keeping a positive image in your mind of the shot you have just seen yourself hit.

Next, and this may be a little tricky to begin with, switch your focus back to the target imprinted on your subconscious so that, although you are looking at the ball, the image of the target is burning brightly in your mind.

All of this takes patience and hard work to get right. You may well use all of the previous information, you may well not. You may add some things of your own that you have found work for you. All of that is of course fine. The important thing is to somehow get yourself into the most comfortable and advantageous position to be both mentally and physically committed to hitting your chosen shot. Having gone through your PSR1, then, and only then, in a state of semi-unconsciousness with only the target on your mind, should you pull the trigger.

Just because the water is calm it doesn't mean that the crocodiles have left. All of that scar tissue is still there. Once mastered, a solid PSR1 will become your best friend – FACT!

PSR2 – post-shot routine

You have made the swing and hit the shot and now you have to deal with its outcome. GOOD, OK, NOT GOOD – remember that?

How was it? It shouldn't matter! Yes, you read that correctly: it shouldn't matter. This is the skill of learning to accept the outcome, no matter what it is. If it was GOOD, well obviously that's great. If it was OK, then that's acceptable so move on satisfied. NOT GOOD is the hard one to accept.

First of all, how damaging was the shot? Is it something that can be recovered from with a high percentage of success, without taking too much of a risk – a bunker or missed fairway, for example?

If it was, accept the challenge with confidence. If it's quite damaging as in a lost ball or an unplayable lie where penalty shots are involved, it becomes a matter of damage limitation. Do not attempt to make some sort of heroic recovery shot. Instead, take your medicine and move on. The time for reflection and analysis is after the round has been completed. Good players don't follow one bad hole with another, let alone one bad shot with another.

The importance of a solid PSR1 and PSR2 is to keep you in the best possible state of mind to play the next shot to the best of your ability. They need to become your "rod and staff".

The whole point of the PSR2 is to release us from the baggage of the shot that has gone before, limiting the build-up of that scar tissue, so just as you have a trigger to enter PSR1 so you need one to leave PSR2.

Once again, this can be anything that works for you. If, as I have suggested, you use the putting on of your glove to activate your PSR 1 why not take the glove off to leave the BUBBLE? Whatever it is, find something that helps you to let go. You will be doing yourself a huge favour.

It's hard but well worth putting in both the time and the effort to build both pre- and post-shot routines. See what works. I promise that, although at times it may seem a little pointless, it will be an enormous help in playing your best golf.

You may not have the physical capacity to match some of your contemporaries but if you build the mental skills and have a strong mind you can still be a force to be reckoned with.

There are all sorts of different ways in which to play this game well. The history books are littered with people who punched above their weight, attributing their achievements to their mental capacities. There are as many who could be classed as underachievers because they failed to reach the heights their ball-striking skills suggested they should.

GOLF IS HARD!

CHAPTER 2

Pulling the trigger

We are now building the knowledge needed to hit any of the nine recognised ball flights. We know that for every shot we hit the ball is given four flight characteristics: SPEED, DIRECTION, LAUNCH ANGLE and SPIN.

We also know that to add SPEED we need quality of strike and club-head acceleration; that DIRECTION is governed by club-face orientation and the path, which is itself dictated by alignment; and that LAUNCH ANGLE is determined principally by the loft on the club face and the angle of attack, which is determined by the plane. If you are in control of these three elements you are in control of the fourth, SPIN, and therefore the master of your own destiny. No longer should you be asking yourself "What happened there?" or "Why did that happen?"

We have all heard it said before, "knowledge is power". As I promised at the very beginning of this book, you are now getting closer to being in charge of your own golf game, to finding *David*.

CHAPTER 3

See it, feel it, roll it, hole it.

Let us begin at the end, so to speak. By the end I mean the business end of the game, the SHORT GAME, and in particular PUTTING. Is it ART or SCIENCE?

If you were reading about putting 30 years ago this chapter might well have read quite differently.

Today, putting is probably the most individual part of the game. There are now far more methods of wielding the "short stick" than were ever recognised as being "acceptable" when I was learning the game.

Back in the day, if ever you came across someone who held the putter in what might be considered an unorthodox manner, say, left hand below right or, as it's called these days, "left hand low", you would have immediately thought, "I'm onto a winner here; they can't putt!"

Not so these days. It is now a case of doing whatever it takes to get the ball in the hole in as few shots as possible, with much less emphasis on style. As I said earlier, golf isn't ice skating and there are no points for style. You need to be efficient in what you do and it doesn't necessarily have to be pretty.

When you consider that, for the majority of putts we hit, the total length of the putting stroke from beginning to end is rarely more than a yard, you wonder why it is looked upon as such a huge challenge. But therein lies the perceived difficulty: it looks a straightforward operation, to hit a ball into hole, and it is, believe me. All the time we are holing putts it is easy. The problems start when we begin to miss them. But if I were to tell you that most golfers hole more putts than they miss, would you believe me? Think about it for a while. How can that be?

If on average you are taking 35 or fewer putts in an 18-hole round you are holing more than you are missing. Does that make sense?

If you take 35 putts per round you are holing more (18) than you are missing (17) and are performing better than what is classed as "regulation" golf of two putts per hole. So every time we single putt we go into credit for balancing the number of shots needed for the long game.

To monitor your putting performance why not give yourself a "putting handicap"? Start by counting your total number of putts per round. Playing 18 holes, allowing two putts per hole, gives you a total of 36 putts per round. Take 36 as your par and for every putt under this give yourself a "plus handicap".

For example, 33 putts would give you a handicap of plus three, 30 putts and you would be plus six. Similarly, if you go above 36 (par) then you go into a minus situation, with 38 putts equalling a minus-two handicap.

Use this method to track your putting performance and you will soon realise how important this part of the game is in reducing your score.

Improving your short game, putting in particular, is the simplest and most effective way to lower your scores – FACT!

So what does it take to become a good putter? First on the list has to be CONFIDENCE. Forget the mechanics of the putting stroke for a while and let us focus on getting the ball into the hole.

Whenever I see a new pupil for a putting lesson I first work on their confidence. Nothing comes close, when building confidence, to seeing the ball going into the hole time after time, every time. I begin by letting pupils hole putts using their own method from no distance at all, let us say the 12in to 18in range. I encourage them and point out that there is nothing too demanding about this task, that they are more than capable of holing putts consistently and that all they have to do is roll the ball towards the hole and in it will go.

I do not see the point of asking a pupil who wants my help to attempt to hole putts which statistically they are going to miss. I begin and end every putting lesson with a few minutes of holing short putts, with the "short" distance relative to each individual's skill levels. The idea behind this is that at the beginning of a lesson we confirm in our psyche that we have the ability to hole short putts, building confidence. Then at the end of the lesson, watching the last few putts go in does the same. It's great for our confidence that our last memories of the lesson are of putts being holed, not missed.

The middle part of the lesson is focused on any particular aspect of putting required, be it technical, to do with the stroke, or maybe speed control or green reading.

When it comes to putting, I do not see anything positive coming from asking pupils to "practice missing".

I also go to great lengths to try to instil in the mindset the possibility that if you have the physical capability to swing the putter not even the width of your stance there is no reason why you cannot become the best putter in the world, at up to, say, three feet. This distance is open to debate and could vary from pupil to pupil. The important thing is getting that positive mindset, building confidence.

The only things that will hold you back are your own expectations.

One of the things that all really good shot-makers have in their armoury is imagination. This is never more evident than in the short game. Positive imagery and visualisation are powerful tools when it comes to our performance. How many times have we berated ourselves saying things like "I knew I was going to do that" or "I knew that was going to happen" when we have hit a shot that hasn't gone as well as we wished. That, I'm afraid, is the self-fulfilling prophecy. It is almost as if you have willed it to happen by your negative thinking.

Probably the most common situation in which this occurs is when we are faced with a shot with which we are not comfortable, for example hitting over water. But take the water away and it is no problem. Why, when the shot is no different? It is because of the negative imagery and chatter going on between our ears when the water is there. It comes back to our PSR1 and running that video that ALWAYS gives us a POSITIVE outcome – SEE IT!

We are in charge of what we think, no one else is, so change that bad habit of negative thinking into a good one of positive thinking.

Not only can we use our mental capacity to help us hole putts but also our sensory skills. Touch and feel, along with visualisation, are prerequisites for all good putters. Can touch and feel be taught? Yes, up to a point, but remember that only you know how you see your shot being played.

In all my years of playing and teaching I have yet to come across anyone who can specifically tell anyone how hard they have to hit a putt for it to move a certain distance.

I liken this to trying to tell someone how hard they need to throw a ball for it to go a certain distance. Is it going to be a hard, fast throw in which the ball will have a very flat trajectory, or will it be more of a higher, more looping trajectory? Or, conversely, ask someone to toss a ball to you, then get them to explain how hard they threw it. Move back a couple of yards then ask them to repeat the throw. Only they will know how hard they tossed the ball. Only when you SEE IT (visualise) will you be able to FEEL IT.

We need to rely on what our eyes see to tell us how hard we need to hit the putt.

Can I now suggest that as part of our putting PSR1 you stand behind the ball on a line through the ball to the hole, where you would usually expect to squat down to read the line of the putt, only this time straddle the line with your feet. Then, holding the putter in your preferred manner while looking at the hole and focusing hard on the target, swing the putter back and forth with a continuous motion, gradually increasing the length of stroke from nothing upwards until your eyes tell you that you have reached the correct length of stroke.

Use this drill on the practice putting green regularly, to hone your distance control. Putt to different parts of the green with no specific target in mind other than the distance you wish the ball to roll. Long-range putting practice should be confined to distance control.

Learn to SEE IT, learn to FEEL IT!

Having the ability to ROLL the ball is another skill that all good putters possess. A good "ROLL" will have the ball travelling over the putting surface and hugging the ground. This is achieved by adding topspin to the ball. Not only will a putt hit with topspin hug the ground, it will also hold its line better.

A sure-fire way to recognise a good roll is to use a line on the golf ball. Mark a line around the equator of the golf ball and set this line so that it is vertical. Then strike the ball with the putter. If the ball rolls with the line maintaining its vertical aspect you have hit the putt true. Any wobbling of the line indicates a mis-strike. The ball will not roll true and will most probably lose speed quickly and deviate from the intended line.

Most of what are considered hole-able putts are missed due to one of the following:

a) The putter face being misaligned to the intended target line.
b) A mis-strike.

Learn to SEE IT, learn to FEEL IT, learn to ROLL IT.

When it comes to HOLE IT there are two things that need to be considered. The first is the pace of the putt, the second its line or direction.

Ideally, these are things you need to think about only when preparing to hit your putt, with the pace being more important than the line or direction in which you hit it.

The "ideal" pace of any putt is a pace that carries the ball 14 inches past the hole should it miss. Struggling to find the optimum speed for putts means you will struggle to find the line on which to hit them if they are anything other than straight. A putt that curves due to the slope of the green will have multiple lines. If it is hit firm the ball will curve less than a putt that is hit more softly. Develop your visualisation skills to read the greens: SEE IT, practice your distance control; FEEL IT, work on improving the quality of strike; ROLL IT, put in the time and effort on these three aspects and you will soon find yourself HOLING IT a lot more often.

Improving your putting is the quickest way to reduce your scores.

SCIENCE

You can improve your visualisation of the line of the putt by noting your surroundings. Begin the procedure of reading the green well before you arrive at the putting surface. Does the green slope down from back to front? if so, and you are short of the hole the putt will be up hill. That's your first clue. Similarly, is the right side of the green higher than the left or vice versa? That will give some indication of whether your putt will be slower than usual if you are putting "up" the green, and whether it will curve, following the slope.

Initially, stand three or four yards behind the ball, looking for a line. A significant curve or break to the putt will be obvious immediately. Walk the distance of the putt, weighing up changes in the slopes, and begin to factor in how the ball will react as it slows down. The slope of the green will have more influence as the putt sheds its speed, so pay particular attention to the last yard of the putt. This is where any "break" will be magnified. I recommend breaking down the putt into three sections to help read any putt over 15ft.

The first section is when the ball is travelling at its quickest and probably not a lot is going to happen. The middle section, depending on the severity of the slope, is where the ball will begin to be influenced. If it is uphill the ball will lose speed more quickly; downhill it will maintain speed. If it is across a slope the ball will begin to break and follow the slope.

The final third is where things can be more dramatic: uphill the ball will come to a premature stop; downhill it will roll further than expected. The ball will also now be curving a lot more aggressively as it loses speed and the slope takes over.

Pay extra attention to the final third. This is where it will all be happening. A ball coming in from the "high" side of the hole is going with the slope, using it to help carry it towards the hole. A ball on the "low" side is being carried away from the hole by the slope – SEE IT.

Experience helps tremendously when determining how hard to hit a putt; it's a case of finding out what works and what doesn't. TOUCH or FEEL is something that is individual to each of us. The science of hitting a putt a certain distance is reliant on three things:

a) How fast was the putter head travelling at the moment of impact?
b) How good was the quality of strike?
c) How quick/slow was the putting surface?

The speed of the putter head is most easily controlled by the length of the putting stroke.

Learn to control the length of your putting stroke so that it goes the same distance back and through either side of the golf ball. The longer the stroke the further the ball will go. What needs to be considered is that the rhythm or tempo of the stroke remains the same – SEE IT, FEEL IT.

29

Use a metronome to help set your stroke to a constant rhythm

For smooth natural acceleration match the length of backswing to that of the throughswing, so that the clubhead travels the same distance both sides of the golf ball

Our ability to ROLL the ball is governed by the rhythm of the stroke and the quality of the strike. A good putter has a smooth, flowing stroke. We can only achieve that if we are relaxed and tension free.

To help gather information on what will be our own best rhythm, download a metronome onto one of your mobile devices and set it to around 60 beats a minute to begin with. Adjust up or down as required until you find what works best for you and practice to the rhythm of the tick tock beat, swinging the putter head back and through.

When it comes to the quality of strike the first thing is to make sure that we are hitting the ball in the centre of the putter, the sweet spot. To help with this stretch a couple of elastic bands a few times around the head of your putter either side of the sweet spot. Give yourself a reasonable margin for error to begin with, gradually reducing the distance between the bands so that you are closing in on the centre of the putter. You will feel a mishit off either elastic band.

Reduce the distance between rubber bands to improve strike quality

Another great practice drill and one that gives immediate feedback on the quality of strike is the "two-ball drill". Take two balls and place one either side of the sweet spot on the putter with just a small gap between them. If you have a line on the balls even better. Place the balls side by side with the lines vertical. The idea is to strike both balls simultaneously so that they run out together. If one ball out-races the other it will have been hit first. If it is the ball nearest the toe of the putter, the face is closing at impact. If it's the heel ball, the putter face is open as it strikes the ball. This is hard, but the closer you can get the balls to run together the squarer the face at impact. If you can get the lines on the balls to go end over end, even better. Challenging, yes, but the reward for seeing those two balls running together is hugely satisfying.

Ideally a putt of around eight to 10ft works well for this drill. Repeat the drill 10 times then hole one putt from the same distance, then repeat the sequence.

Two ball putting drill. One ball on toe of putter the other on heel

How we hold the putter has a tremendous influence on our performance. Not too many years ago you would have been advised to use what is known as "the reverse overlap" grip. In a conventional grip the little finger of the bottom (right) hand overlaps the forefinger of our top (left) hand. In a reverse overlap grip this is reversed, only in this case the forefinger of the left hand points down to the ground, covering the fingers of the right hand.

Nowadays, there are far more acceptable ways to hold the putter. Each has its merits and I suggest you do a little research to find out which one you feel most comfortable with. For me, it is preferable to use a neutral hold similar to that for the long game, in which the hands are linked in some way, the palms of the hands face one another and the back of the top hand and palm of the bottom hand face the target.

Our set-up for putting tends to be a condensed version of the set-up we use for the long game.

For a neutral, comfortable set-up, take your normal long-game set-up and narrow your stance so that the distance between the outside of your two feet is shoulder width. Remember that for the long game, it is the distance between the insides of your two feet.

Tilt from your hips – this will be at a greater angle than that in your long-game set-up, because the club is now comparatively short – and let your arms hang down directly below your shoulders.

Drop your head so that you are now looking directly at the ground. The lines across your feet, knees, hips, forearms and shoulders need to be parallel to the ball-to-target line.

Your eyes should be directly over the ball when it is on the putting green; I see this as non-debatable. Stand as suggested, hold a ball on the bridge of your nose and let it drop. Wherever it hits the ground is where the ball needs to be positioned, i.e. directly beneath your eye-line in the centre of your stance. To find out what works best I simply say "Watch and learn from the best."

Often, the length of our putting stroke will rarely exceed a yard from start to finish. From that we can assume that the motion is quite a compact and simple one to execute; it looks easy and trust me, it is. All you are doing is swinging the putter head around the width of your stance. Good putters, like good ball strikers, have much in common when it comes to the putting stroke, with the movement usually coming from the shoulders. A putting stroke with quiet hands is far more preferable to one in which the hands are active.

I tend to think of a solid putting stroke as having a "lock-and-rock" motion. To achieve this, "lock" the upper part of your arms to the side of your chest and "rock" your shoulders. This locking/rocking motion comes from the same family as the letter Y when talking about the long game. It holds everything together and will give you a path for the putter head similar to that for the long game – circular, but more subtle.

I regard this type of stroke as a "connected, gated stroke". Using the natural path of the putter you "open the gate" on the backswing. The putter face will begin to look marginally to the right as the putter head comes back on the inside. Using the natural in-to-in path you "close the gate" through impact and the putter face ends the stroke looking left of target. Putting with an in-to-in gated stroke keeps the face square to the path.

There are those who might well advocate a "straight back, straight through" style of stroke. That's fine. All I would ask is how far back and through can you move the putter head without manipulating the face? At some point, your putter head will come inside the line. If you putt straight back, straight through or up and down the line, as it is sometimes referred to, more often than not you end up with a "shut-to-open" manipulation of the putter face.

This manipulation comes at a cost – remember, there is always a trade-off. With me, it's the lack of consistency that this method breeds. But, as the underlying theme of this book is that there is more than one way to play, try both methods and see which you feel more comfortable with and which, more importantly, performs best. You will probably find they are one and the same.

What I will add here is that there are designs of putters which suit one or other putting style. If you use a gated stroke, a heel-and-toe weighted or blade-type putter will suit better. If you prefer the straight back, straight through, up-and-down-the-line style, one of the more exotic spaceship or mallet designs will suit better. However, as putting is mostly about confidence, when choosing a putter first pick one up and ask yourself, "Do I like the look of this one?" and then, "Can I hole putts with it?" – ROLL IT.

With all the hard work done let's now HOLE IT.

We have weighed up all the options regarding reading the green, taking into account the slopes. We have practiced our stroke while looking at the hole and have chosen the line, which is dependent on the speed.

Once the line is chosen I suggest finding a point on the putting green, only a yard or two in front of you, over which the ball needs to roll. Holding the putter in your right hand only, place the putter behind the ball taking great care to correctly aim the putter at the point on the ground you have just chosen. Then complete your set-up.

Have one last look at the hole, visualising the ball tracking along the chosen line at the chosen speed before finally disappearing. Then, and this is the hard part, pull the trigger. You have done all you can; once the ball is struck it is completely beyond your control. Learn to accept that not all good putts go in and that there is always a trade-off: sometimes you will get either the line and the speed wrong or maybe both and the ball still goes in.

SEE IT, FEEL IT, ROLL IT, HOLE IT, art or science? Neither. It's GOLF!

Chapter 4

Club captain elect!

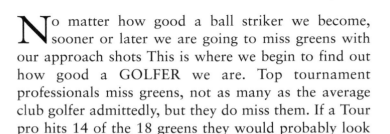

No matter how good a ball striker we become, sooner or later we are going to miss greens with our approach shots This is where we begin to find out how good a GOLFER we are. Top tournament professionals miss greens, not as many as the average club golfer admittedly, but they do miss them. If a Tour pro hits 14 of the 18 greens they would probably look back and think that on that particular occasion they hit the ball OK.

It's what they do when they miss a green that sets them apart from the rest. More often than not they will chip and then putt only once, somehow turning three shots into two. Throw the occasional chip in into the mix and it's easy to see where the old saying "drive for show, putt for dough" comes from.

When it comes to chipping or pitching, what should we be aware of? First, keep it simple. In all my years of playing, watching and teaching I have yet to come across anyone who is trying to make the game more difficult than it needs to be. Yet whenever I see a high-handicap amateur miss a green and the first club they pull from the bag is some sort of wedge I think *Noooooo!* fine if you need loft to get over some sort of obstacle or hazard but completely unnecessary if there is no trouble between you and the flag.

The first message I try to get across to anyone who struggles with their chipping is MORE LOFT, MORE RISK.

The rules state that we are allowed to carry up to 14 clubs. I see that as an opportunity to use any one of 13 of them where necessary. For chipping from around the green I wouldn't recommend the driver, as the head is too big. But that is only my opinion; there is nothing in the rules to say that certain clubs HAVE to be used in certain situations. The putter is recommended for use on the green as it gives us the best chance of holing the ball, but it is not compulsory. You may get some ugly looks from the greenkeeper if you do use another club, but it is solely your choice.

Here is a true story that highlights misconceptions.

Many years ago I was giving a joint lesson to two people. They were both members of a club, not where I was coach I hasten to add, had handicaps and had been playing for a number of years. The husband of one of the players later became club captain.

The lesson in question was on the short game – chipping to be precise. I asked them to pull out their favourite club and begin chipping a few balls towards the hole. Their performances weren't great, but fair enough, they were here to learn. My first question to them was on their club selection. The chip shot in question called for a straightforward chip and run with probably a six, seven or eight iron, but both players had pulled out a wedge.

"Why the wedge?" I asked. "Why not a seven or eight iron?"

"I mustn't use that," one of the players responded. "I have to use a wedge. My husband tells me that that is the rule."

"What do you mean, that is the rule?"

"That's what he says. If you are just off the green you HAVE to use a wedge."

True story, I kid you not.

Needless to say, they were soon pointed in the right direction and both players went on to become tidy golfers with very solid short games.

Whatever it takes, then. The job in hand is to get the ball into the hole in the fewest shots, so if you haven't any hazards, I recommend going into the middle of the bag for your choice of club. Learn to love this club and stick with it for your straightforward chip-and-run shots around the green. More loft equals more risk!

The basic chip shot is straightforward enough to execute and is more aligned with the putting game than the long game. The only addition to the advice I would add to that for putting is to put more body weight on your lead leg, place your hands lower down the grip and open out your body alignment so that you are facing the target a little more, with a small amount of forward shaft lean so that your hands are just ahead of the ball.

Seven iron pitch and run. Weight on lead leg. Arms and shaft form letter Y, lock and rock

Stance slightly open to target line

Target line

To execute the shot adopt the "lock and rock" routine, favouring your left side with your body weight throughout. Let the natural loft of the club get the ball into the air and land it on the green so that it runs like a putt towards the hole.

Above all, don't be like the club captain elect.

There are no rules when it comes to club selection, there are only "advisories". I often wonder how good a captain he became.

Finally, another true tale. A pupil asked if I could cut down to putter length an old hybrid club so that it could be used around the green – whatever it takes!

The alternative to the chip and run is the "lofted pitch", sometimes called the "lob" or "parachute" shot. This is the one that comes in useful when we have some sort of obstacle to negotiate on our way to the hole and we need a greater degree of launch and a decent angle for the shot. The basic requirement for this shot is more loft. We have already learned that the biggest influence on launch angle is the loft manufactured into the design of the club. We now need to pull out one of the most lofted clubs in the bag, if not the club that is most lofted. Experience will help in your club choice.

These days, the selection of wedges available means that there is a club out there that has been designed for pretty well every eventuality. The loft is of great benefit when playing these short, soft landing approach shots but there is another design feature that needs to be factored into our choice of club: the "BOUNCE". This is a design feature that is built into the club and that does exactly what it says on the tin: it is there to help the club skim or BOUNCE across the surface of the grass without it digging in.

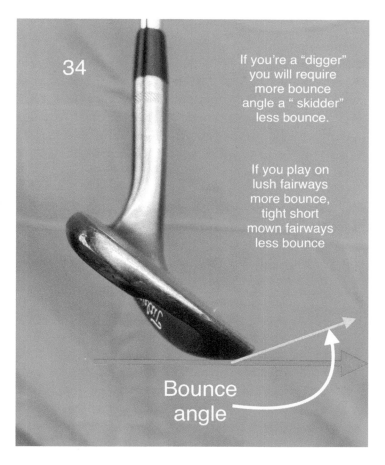

34

If you're a "digger" you will require more bounce angle a " skidder" less bounce.

If you play on lush fairways more bounce, tight short mown fairways less bounce

Bounce angle

If you look at the sole of your wedges you will find that there is some sort of radius or curvature to them. It is this curvature that is referred to as the BOUNCE and if used correctly it can help tremendously to enhance your ability to play the pitch shots with confidence.

To put my club-fitting hat on for a moment, if you tend to play more on a parkland course where the grass is quite lush, or if your angle of attack is quite steep, you will fare better with a high BOUNCE angle. In a shallower angle of attack or if you are playing on a links type of course where the ball lies a lot tighter to the grass, a lower BOUNCE angle will be more suitable.

The technique required to play these pitch shots now moves away from the putting and chipping family and more into the long-game aspect of shot making. Let me talk you through the alterations to the set-up required to play these shots.

Take your stance so that the club face is square to the target line and your feet parallel to the target line. Widen your stance and widen it again so that your feet are a similar distance apart to that when using a driver. Flair out your left foot so that your toes are turned towards the target, and squat a little as if you are sat into your stance. Shift your body weight well over your lead leg so that your left knee is directly above your left foot.

The ball should be directly below your sternum, as this is where the low point of your swing will fall.

Drop your hands to a lower position than you would normally adopt. This will decrease the angle between your arms and the golf shaft from that which you would have in an orthodox set up. Your hands should be directly opposite the golf ball and shaft in a neutral position, giving neither positive nor negative shaft lean.

The swing itself is generated with an upper-body-connected rotation. The low hands will encourage an early wrist hinge. The wide stance will afford stability in the swing, with the body weight remaining on the lead leg throughout. An early committed release with the club head accelerating in the downswing will bring the shaft back into that neutral position at impact, imparting maximum loft onto the ball. The early release pattern will use the BOUNCE to help to prevent the leading edge from digging into the ground.

The acceleration of the club head through impact will impart the SPIN that will give you the control.

35

Lofted pitch
Wide stance
weight on
lead leg left
foot flared,
no forward
shaft
lean
(Neutral)
Ball directly
below
Sternum

Target
line

If you have missed the green and neither the pitch and run nor the lofted pitch are the "go to shot", the odds are that you are in a bunker. The green-side bunker shot becomes quite simple and straightforward and should hold no fear if we stick to some basic guidelines. After all, it's the only shot in which we don't have to hit the ball. In fact, if we do hit the ball when playing this shot, we have made some sort of major error in our execution of it.

The first objective of any bunker shot is to get the ball out. You may well come across a situation in which you have to play away from the hole. Should this be the case, take your medicine and remember that golf is damage limitation; every time you hit the ball it counts against you.

Club selection for this one is usually fairly simple: usually you would choose the most lofted.

As with all golf shots, the key to a successful outcome is the set-up. The bunker shot is no exception, and the vast selection of wedges now available makes this shot so much more straightforward.

Years ago, if you were looking for advice on how to play any sort of high-launching pitch or bunker shot, you would have been given the following information, or something very similar.

"Square the club face to the target line. If it's a bunker shot settle your feet into the sand with your stance open (aiming left of target). This sets the club face open to the path. Place the ball forward in your stance and swing in the direction in which you are set up, i.e. across the line out-to-in."

This advice is old school, however, because previously, only a limited loft was available on clubs. It used to be that a sand iron, the most lofted club at 52 degrees, was all that was available. This meant that to add loft the club face had to be opened. Now we know that an open face is aiming right. Therefore, to bring the face back into a position in which it is square to the target line we must shift our body alignment to the left.

You can't get away from the fact that it works. It has done for many years and I'm sure there are those who will continue to play this type of shot this way. But is it the most effective and simple method and if I were to come up with something more straightforward, would you consider it?

A brief overview of the aforementioned technique gives us a method whereby we are essentially playing a shot that with a less lofted club would produce a left-to-right ball flight, either a fade or slice depending on the severity of the separation between face and path.

On landing, we might well find that the ball kicked to the right., due to the clockwise spin that had been imparted. This would make the roll out more difficult to read.

Question – does it make sense to aim the face in one direction and swing the club in another? In my opinion, no.

Is there a more simple and logical way to play this shot? In my opinion, yes.

Let's go back a few pages to the "lofted pitch shot" and use this method for a bunker shot. Now that there are clubs available with anything up to 64 degrees of loft we have no need to "open" the face; we have all the loft we need already built into the club. This improvement, along with the understanding of how the BOUNCE can be used, makes this shot so much simpler.

We can get set up with a more orthodox club face and body alignment and swing the club along the same neutral lines as those we would use in a conventional shot. The only additional advice I would give if you are playing a lofted pitch shot as opposed to a green-side bunker shot is to settle your feet into the sand.

The reasons for this are twofold: first, the position of your feet impacts where the low point of the swing falls. It will now be situated well below the level of the sand on which the ball is sitting, the club head will enter the sand behind the ball and there will be no need for any attempt to get below the ball in order to dig it out. The low point has been preset in your set-up.

Second, as you must really commit to the shot and accelerate the club through the sand, you will have a more stable platform from which you can swing and there will be less chance of your feet slipping on the unstable sand.

This position makes a lot more sense and seems more logical, enabling you to get set up and swing towards the target as opposed to across the target line. It also means that the ball will not have any slice or side spin to kick it off to the right on landing.

36

Bunker splash
shot
As per lofted
pitch, plus feet
lowered into
sand a little &
hands lowered
at address
creating
greater
"acute" angle

Target
line

CHAPTER 5

You can talk to a fade!

A good many people think that the Holy Grail of golf shots is the straight one. Trust me, that is the hardest one to hit.

Good golfers control their ball flight by imparting spin onto the ball, as mentioned earlier. As a golfer's ball-striking skills develop they will notice that, due to their "default swing", a certain "default shot" shape will become more prevalent. It may be left to right – fade/slice, or right to left – draw/hook, depending on the severity of curvature. If it isn't either of these, all that is left is a push – straight right, or a pull – straight left.

Any separation between face and path will bring about a shot that will curve. The bigger the separation the bigger the curve.

To recap from earlier, for a shot that curves to the right the face is "OPEN" to the path, and for one that curves to the left the face is "CLOSED" to the path.

A straight shot is hit with a club face that is square to the path.

Now unless we have the patience of Jobe, more time on our hands than we know what do with or is good for us and commitment bordering on brain damage I suggest we work with our "default swing" to produce our "default shot" the majority of the time.

It is well documented that it takes up to 10,000 hours of structured practice and tuition for anyone to reach their potential in any given skill, be it playing golf, learning a musical instrument, playing chess, table tennis or whatever. My schoolboy maths tells me that that equates to approximately three hours a day every day for nine years.

Now, if you fancy putting in that amount of time and effort in your quest for the "Holy Grail" of the straight shot go right ahead. Personally I think your time and effort would be better spent learning to accept that our "default swing" is probably our biggest strength not our greatest weakness. It is, after all, the "factory setting" with which we are born.

Remember, playing good golf is all about damage limitation, so, forgetting the Holy Grail for a moment, which of the nine recognised ball flights is going to be the least damaging to our performance and the easiest to consistently re-produce?

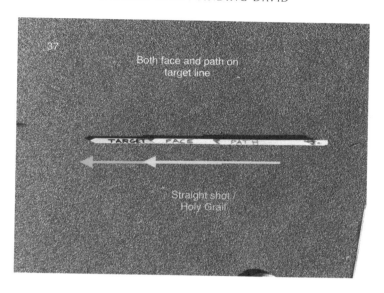

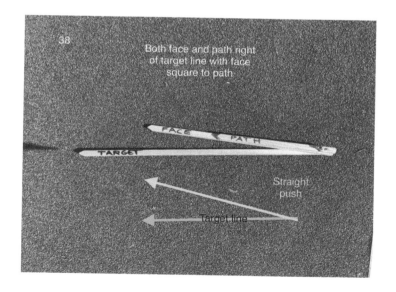

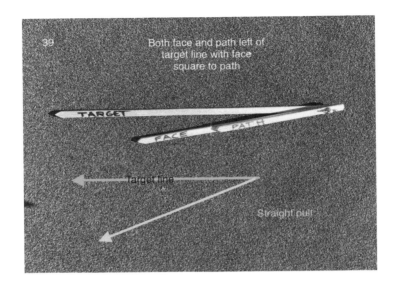

39 Both face and path left of
target line with face
square to path

TARGET

FACE   PATH

Target line

Straight pull

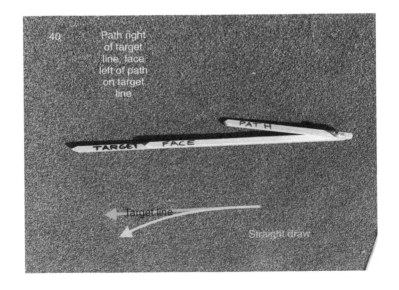

40 Path right
of target
line, face
left of path
on target
line

PATH

TARGET FACE

Target line

Straight draw

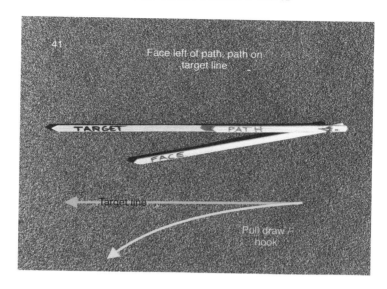

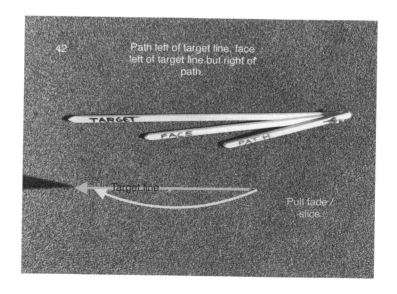

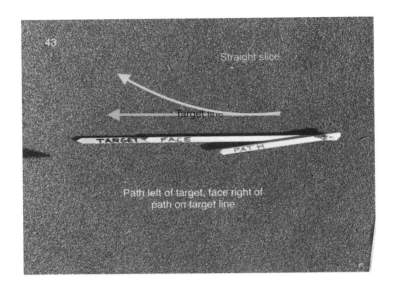

43

Straight slice

Target line

TARGET FACE PATH

Path left of target, face right of
path on target line

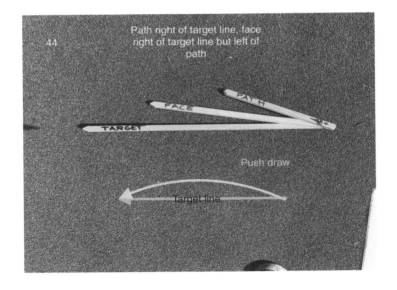

44

Path right of target line, face
right of target line but left of
path

PATH

FACE

TARGET

Push draw

Target line

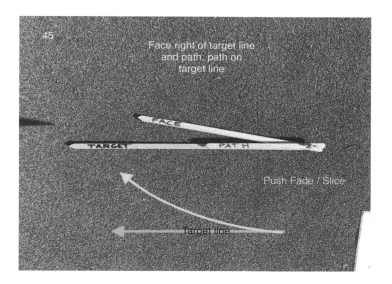

It is the one that is the easiest for us to produce and then repeat. This gives us the consistency we all crave. But why is it the least damaging? Because we can build that shot into our pre-shot routine. If we can predict where the ball will go and how it will get there, our confidence levels will rise exponentially and the fear of failure will be taken away.

For some reason, the fade has always been looked upon as the poor relation when it comes to the preferred ball flight, and the draw was always the sign of a good ball striker. Golf courses used to ring to the sound of "He/She is a good player. Have you seen the way he/she draws the ball?"

Not so much these days, though. It has now become trendier to play with a fade. I see this as a spin off from the main professional golf tours in which the great players on these tours now hit the ball so far that they are happy to give up the few extra yards a draw gives them in favour of the control gained by hitting the fade.

Or to put it another way, "You can talk to a fade, but a hook doesn't listen." With the cut spin that creates the fade the ball will fly a little higher, a little shorter and land softer than it will with a draw, in which the spin is more aligned to an overspin, which will make the ball kick on a little when landing. Hence, "You can talk to a fade" asking it to "sit down" when it lands, but "a hook doesn't listen", a hook being an aggressive draw that will go the extra distance due to the lack of control. The manufacture of these two ball flights comes down to our understanding of the relationship between path and face.

To improve your control of the fade or draw go through the following practice drill.

With a five or six iron take up your orthodox set-up position. Make quarter swings with your usual amount of forearm rotation, gradually adding length to the swing, from quarter to half to full, noting the ball flight.

Then go through the same process again but this time "weaken" your hold on the club. Remember that in this context "weaken" refers to the position of the hands on the club not the tension with which we are holding it.

Once again, begin with quarter swings, gradually adding length to them, only this time reducing the amount of forearm rotation in both the down and through swing. Note the ball flight. It should show signs of having some amount of left-to-right curvature. Once again, systematically add length to the swing.

You should begin to see and then feel the result of how the weakened hold and lack of forearm rotation alters the relationship between face and path, leaving the face open to path at impact and imparting the left-to-right or clockwise spin giving you a left-to-right ball flight. The open face has also added loft, hence the higher ball flight.

Repeat the process, only this time "strengthen" your hold on the club. Add forearm rotation in the down and through swing. The extra forearm activity will reduce the loft, closing the club face through impact and generating a lower, more penetrating ball flight that will curve left. By either increasing or reducing the amount of forearm rotation, coupled with the appropriate re-positioning of the hands, we can guarantee a specific ball flight.

The "Holy Grail" is the hardest to hit because the margins are so fine. Too much or too little manipulation of the club face through the rotating forearms and hand placement can produce either fade or draw. There is very little margin for error and you run the risk of developing a two-way miss. The ball could go any one of three ways – straight, curve right or curve left. By learning to control the club face via the forearms and hands you are controlling the spin, be it either a fade or draw spin. Whichever you find the easiest to repeat becomes you "default shot".

Now that we know how to make a ball curve at will, we need to get the ball to finish on target.

Let's go back to an orthodox set-up with a middle iron, club face square to the target line, neutral hold and body alignment parallel to the target line. Once we introduce the ball we have a reference point for our circle. Ideally the club path will meet the ball at the point at which our circle and target line intersect. In effect, the target line becomes a tangent to the circle.

By using our circle to describe the path the club head takes, which ideally is in-to-in, we can easily see how, if we move the ball further forward in the stance (closer to the target), the circle and consequently the path of the club begins to go left. By the same token, moving the ball back in the stance (further away from the target) the circle/path becomes right of target.

With that knowledge and the skill to control the club face through hand positioning and forearm rotation, we can alter our set-up and manipulate our swing path to produce either a right-to-left (fade /slice) or left-to-right (draw/hook) ball flight.

The correct ball positioning is paramount to being in control of golf shots. Unfortunately, there are no hard and fast rules. This comes under the heading of DEBATABLE but you need to be aware that the further back in the stance the ball is the greater the opportunity for it to go right, and the further forward it is the more likely it is to go left.

For an orthodox golf shot the window for the correct ball positioning is opposite your left toe for the driver, the longest club, and in the middle of the stance for the shortest, the wedge. All other the suitable ball positions fall within that range.

Ball positioning is generic. Golf is not an exact science. Precise ball positioning is very much an individual thing that is easily worked out once you understand the cause and effect of the face-to-path relationship.

Each of the swings used to hit either a fade or draw will most probably contain one of the following two elements, which are relatively easy to spot even to the untrained eye.

The fade swing will most probably end up with what might be described as a sawn off or curtailed follow through. This is because the release pattern of the hands has been minimised, due to the reduction of forearm rotation, resulting in the club head being held off from overtaking the hands through impact.

As you would expect, the opposite occurs when hitting a draw shot. The extra activity in the forearms encourages a more fluid, longer follow though, resulting in the club being wrapped fully around the back of your neck.

Does the shot determine the swing or the swing the shot? It's an interesting thought.

CHAPTER 6

Hit it high, watch it fly.
Hit it low, watch it go.

Ever wanted to hit a high shot over a tree and needed a nine iron for the launch angle but a seven iron to achieve the distance? I know I have.

The obvious solution is to open everything up and hit a fade. We know a fade hits the ball higher, but what if a fade doesn't suit? What if we have to hit it straight ? Or we need to flight the ball higher to take advantage of a strong following wind

Once again, let's look to our set-up. First move the ball forwards in the stance, so that you eliminate any forward shaft lean, exposing the maximum loft on the club face to the ball at impact. Relax your grip pressure a little and take it down a couple of notches to somewhere around three. This allows your wrists to hinge more quickly in the backswing, giving you a steeper angle of attack. Your swing shape will alter ever so slightly to become more of a V-shape. The ball will launch more steeply and reach its peak height sooner.

What if we want to keep the ball flight down, to keep it under the low-hanging branches of a tree, or hit into a stiff wind and minimise the wind's effect on the ball?

If you are comfortable with the adjustments made to hit the higher shot let's make similar changes but in the opposite direction. Instead of moving the ball forwards in the stance, move it back. The greater shaft lean will de-loft the club. Your seven iron will now turn into something resembling a six or even a five. Increase your grip pressure a couple of notches, from four to six. This will stifle the wrist hinge and give more of a U shape to your swing and a shallower angle of attack. This will send the ball out faster with a lower, more penetrating ball flight.

Golf can be a simple and logical game once we have learned to understand what effect the four basic elements of SPEED, DIRECTION, LAUNCH ANGLE and SPIN have on the ball. Note that I said SIMPLE not EASY. There is a huge difference.

PART FOUR

Myelin or Merlin

Chapter 1

Fact or fiction

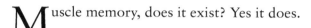

M uscle memory, does it exist? Yes it does.

Practice builds muscle memory, which allows us to carry out tasks more subconsciously and efficiently. "The more I practice the luckier I become" is a well-known phrase when it comes to golf improvement. It works fine as long as we are practising the right things in the correct manner.

You should by now have picked up enough technical information to be able to move your golf along a logical and structured pathway, to be able to perform better by carefully managing alterations to your default swing.

We build muscle memory by practising SLOWLY, not in real time. We have been doing this since the day we were born so it is a skill we already possess, even though we may not know it. The basis of muscle memory is a chemical myelin, - it impacts on every muscle movement that we make from blinking and breathing to swinging a golf club.

Myelin is a form of insulation that wraps around nerves. Its presence speeds up the transmission of messages from our brains to our muscles. Basically, the more often we carry out a task the more myelin is produced and the clearer the message.

When we were young, how many times did we fall over when learning to walk, or miss our mouths when trying to feed ourselves? It was because we hadn't produced enough myelin to build the muscle memory. We humans only really produce myelin from birth, hence the steep learning curve in our early years.

The amazing thing about myelin is that you still produce it no matter how quickly or SLOWLY you go through a muscle movement. So, if you are trying to fix that path for your back swing or working on that transition or a specific release pattern to hit a draw, go through the necessary swing motion required in slow motion. SEE IT then FEEL IT and GROOVE IT, with the help of myelin.

The world's best ice skaters have probably fallen over more times than anyone else but keep getting up, practising not until they get it right but until they don't get it wrong!

Chapter 2

Range rats

It's pretty safe to say that in this day and age most golf clubs or courses have practice facilities of some sort or another, be they a putting green with a short-game area, a practice ground where you hit then pick up your own balls or a fully-fledged driving range where the balls are supplied. That means that there is very little excuse for not putting the time in, should you have the time of course.

This brings me to another true story of a pupil who came to me for lessons. looking for the "secret."

Things were going quite nicely and steady progress was being made in multiple areas. We were on course for the pupil to reach his goal until this one particular lesson when he showed up and informed me that he had ceased practising because it had become boring.

This was totally unexpected. Up until this point he had been the perfect pupil, totally committed to the process, his handicap coming down and improving results to show for his efforts.

"Oh, right," I said. "Can I take it from that that everything is now sorted, that every shot is going exactly where you want it? Every drive, every iron shot, every putt, that you have total control of your golf ball for every shot you hit?"

"I wish," he answered. "No, far from it. I'm not sure where the next one is going."

"OK, you're not sure where the next one is going and you find that boring."

"Yes."

"If every shot was perfect with no room for improvement I would call that boring. If I was unsure as to the outcome, I would call that interesting; every shot would become an adventure."

I told him that the "secret" he was looking for was down on the ground in front of him, or, as Ben Hogan, one of the best ball strikers ever, put it "The secret is in the dirt."

Let's assume that you choose to practice at a driving range. How do you structure the time and how many balls do you hit?

One the first things I try to stress to all my pupils is that, regardless of the facility, they should treat practice as they would a game out on the course. Take your time hitting balls – say, 30 balls hit with focus, will be far more beneficial than 100 balls hit quick fire. Place the balls a reasonable distance from the point on the ground from which they are to be struck, to make you move to collect a ball for the next shot. That way, you can go through your PSR1 and PSR2 for every shot.

ALWAYS place alignment aids on the ground to act as a reference for your set-up, one representative of the ball-to-target line, another parallel to this to aid stance alignment, and another running across the inner one forming a right angle representative of the ball position.

Have a definite plan for each session and stick to it regardless. Do not get sidetracked.

Always take DEAD AIM at your target. NEVER hit a shot without having a target or specific goal in mind.

Begin by hitting a few warm-up shots. A wedge is probably the most popular choice of club here. Avoid the temptation to pull out the driver to begin with.

If you're planning a long session, anything over 30 balls, have a break, clear your head and refocus.

Too many times I have seen golfers, range rats as I call them, rushing to hit as many balls as possible in the time they have, pulling out the driver at the start and hitting balls with a fire-and-forget approach. They hit maybe 100-plus balls, with no thought or structure, convincing themselves that they are practising and wondering why there is no improvement.

Remember, it's 10,000 hours of structured, focused, applied commitment that is required. Hitting balls ad-hoc, no matter how many, doesn't do it.

Myelin can work either for or against you, so practice with purpose, make the practice worthwhile.

Here are three practice sessions which can be used as and when they are appropriate for your needs. I have found these to be most beneficial in helping pupils structure their practice time.

Session one will probably take around 30 minutes. I see this as the warm-up. This is the one that will help you most if you struggle to take your game from the range to the course.

Session two should take around an hour so and should be used as an extended warm-up or a cooling-off session after a game.

Session three is around the three-hour mark so should be used as a stand-alone practice.

Session 1, approximately 30 minutes

1 x chip shot, wedge 10 yds
1 x short wedge, 30 yds
1 x half wedge, 50–70 yds
1 x full wedge, 70–100 yds

* * * * * * * * * * * *

1 x chip, 6 iron
1 x short, 6 iron
1 x half, 6 iron
1 x full, 6 iron

* * * * * * * * * * * *

3 x 8 iron
3 x 6 iron
3 x 4 iron
3 x hybrid/rescue wood
3 x 3 wood
3 x drivers
1 x wedge – full
1 x wedge – half
1 x wedge – short

6 iron – hit five shots to a specific target, review session and record any positive/negative information in notebook to present to coach.

Session 2, approximately 1 hour

3 x chip shot, wedge 10 yds
3 x short wedge, 30 yds
3 x half wedge, 50–70 yds
3 x full wedge, 70–100 yds

* * * * * * * * * * *

5 shots with each club – 9 iron to 4 iron
5 shots with each club – hybrid/rescue, 3 wood & driver.
10 minutes hitting 6 iron – target focused.

* * * * * * * * * * *

Choose club based on recent performance.
10 focused shots to target and record data

* * * * * * * * * * *

Final fun session
Clubs of choice, target-focused, approximately 10 minutes.

Review and record data in notebook and present to coach.

Session 3, approximately 3 hours

5 x chip shot – wedge, 10 yds
5 x short wedge, 30 yds
5 x half wedge, 50–70 yds
5 x full wedge, 70–100yds

* * * * * * * * * * *

Irons

10 shots with each club 9 iron to 4 iron
20 x 7 iron to target
20 x 5 iron to target
Record data

* * * * * * * * * * *

Woods

10 x shots hybrid/rescue
10 x shots 3 wood
10 x shots driver
10 x shots with driver into fairway width target.

Record positive/negative data to present to coach.

* * * * * * * * * * *

Shot-shaping fun session

10 minutes, club of your choice, you call the shots. High – low – fade – draw.

* * * * * * * * * * * *

Imaginary 18 holes – own course.

Hit each shot as if playing your own course, allowing two putts per hole. Count your score.

Warm down and stretch after lengthy practice session. Record data and present to coach for evaluation.

CHAPTER 3

The "ugly zone"

It can become difficult at times to see any improvement in your performance despite all the practice. Reward can seem a long way off. This is when we are in the "ugly zone". Nothing goes right despite all your efforts. The only way out of the ugly zone is to keep walking, just one step at a time with small incremental improvements along the way.

These small improvements can be difficult to monitor, though. How do we know we are improving without the results to prove it?

Start by creating a log: number of fairways hit, if missed was it left or right. Number of greens hit in regulation, if missed was it left or right. Short or long, how many putts per round. If a green is missed, how many shots to get up and down. This will form the basis of your route out of the ugly zone.

A minute improvement in all aspects of your game will pay large overall dividends. For example, if a Tour pro were to save just half a shot per round that's two shots per tournament, the difference between winning and maybe finishing tenth, or making and missing a cut, or keeping or losing your Tour card – all very fine margins.

A great way to help take your practice-ground game to the course, and let's face it, we all probably need help with that, is to set ourselves goals or challenges.

This series of challenges can be customised for different handicaps and works well.

Example 1

Hit six fairways with a tee shot
Hit eight greens in regulation
Do not three putt on the front nine.
Par holes 15, 16, 17 and 18
Two birdies in the round
Single putt one of the first six greens.

For handicap 0–4 complete all six tasks
For handicap 4–9 complete four tasks
For handicap 10–18 complete three tasks
For handicap 18–24 complete two tasks
For handicap 24 plus complete one task

To be used for all groups of six challenges.

* * * * * * * * * * * *

Example 2

Five single putts per round
No more than two bunkers on front nine
Two chip and one putt in the round
Hit the first par-three green with tee shot
Par holes 8, 9, 10,16, 17, 18
No three putts in the last six holes

* * * * * * * * * * * *

Example 3

Hit all par-three greens with tee shots
Par stroke index one.
Two birdies on back nine
No bunkers on back nine
Hit first fairway
Hit last fairway

Example 4

Birdie one par five
Birdie one par four
No water in first six holes
No three putts on front nine
Single putt either holes eight, nine, ten and eleven
Hit two par-three greens with tee shot.

* * * * * * * * * * * *

Example 5

No lost ball
No more than two bunkers on back nine
Hit eight fairways with tee shots
Single putt two of the last six greens
Birdie one par three
Hit three greens in regulation on back nine

* * * * * * * * * * * *

All of those are examples of how you can make up challenges to suit your needs. The list can be endless; the important thing is to log the results. By constantly challenging yourself with each set of tasks you will find that your mindset will alter just as it did when it changed from making swings to hitting shots. Now it will change from hitting shots to making a score.

PART FIVE

Lead dog

That pretty much concludes *Default Golf*. I sincerely hope that you have enjoyed the journey.

As it is with life in general, the golfing journey is never a straight line along a road. It is a more colourful trip through country lanes, turning here, turning there, backtracking and adjusting, taking wrong turns and learning from them.

We start off with our basic goal and a simple template of how to achieve it. Along the way we encounter bumps, potholes and diversions. We avoid the bumps and potholes and take the necessary diversions, and all of the time have our end goal in mind.

When we do deviate from our chosen path we need to rectify our course, but be mindful that this correction may well be overdone. For example, we would never consider taking a whole bottle of painkillers to try and alleviate a headache when experience has taught us that only two would be sufficient for the cure.

So it is with golf. Advice is offered as a dose of medicine. But like the painkillers it can be overdone, in which case we go from being off course in one direction and rectifying it, only to find that we have overdone the cure and are off in another direction.

Imagine the journey a sailor takes when repeatedly tacking and following a zigzag route into a headwind, continually crossing the most direct route in order to reach the final destination. This pretty much sums up everyone's golfing journey.

I sincerely hope that as you have made it this far you have enjoyed this part of your golfing journey. I promise you it is by no means the end of the road; it might just be one of those moments when you decide to "tack" and go off in another direction.

We may look for perfection but how about we settle for progress? It makes our journey much more pleasurable and our goals much more attainable.

This book has been 40 years in the writing. It came about following suggestions from some wonderful clients who put their trust in me to help them with their golf. I wouldn't dare to think of myself as being so pretentious that every lesson I gave was a complete success, but what I would like to think is that from every lesson I have given the pupil did manage to take away something that benefitted them, even if it was only a biology lesson on the effectiveness of myelin.

They say that if things don't change, they stay as they are, or to quote Einstein, "To keep doing the same things and expect different results is one of the first signs of insanity."

Never has this been truer than in our quest for improvement, be it golf or anything else in life. So be brave, make the decision and stick to the process. It's progress not perfection that we look for so become the lead dog, because unless you do the view will never change.

Happy golfing, now go and find DAVID!!!!!

Lightning Source UK Ltd.
Milton Keynes UK
UKHW051351040122
396237UK00007B/133/J